Chicken

Chicken

Sue Ashworth

Jacqueline Bellefontaine

Jennie Berresford

Joanna Craig

Jill Eggleton

Nicola Fowler

Carole Handslip

Jane Hartshorn

Kathryn Hawkins

Cara Hobday

Deh-ta Hsiung

Wendy Lee

Louise Steele

Rosemary Wadey

Pamela Westland

p

This is a Parragon book
This edition published in 2001

Parragon
Queen Street House
4 Queen Street
Bath, BA1 1HE UK

Copyright © Parragon 1998

ISBN: 0-75256-664-4 (Paperback)
ISBN: 0-75256-668-7 (Hardback)

Printed in China

Edited, designed and produced by Haldane Mason, London

Update and cover design by The Bridgewater Book Company

Acknowledgements
Editor: Anne Hildyard
Design: dap ltd
Photographer: St John Asprey (for pages 22, 23–24, 26–30, 32–35, 39, 55–61,
62–68, 72–73, 74, 75, 76–79, 80–88, 89, 91, 106–113, 115–119, 130, 131–134, 135–139, 140–147,
153–157, 158–161, 166–167, 182–194, 195, 207, 216, 217–219)
Home Economist: Jacqueline Bellefontaine (*for above pages*)
Other Photography: Karl Adamson, Sue Atkinson, Iain Bagwell, Martin Brigdale,
Amanda Heywood, Joff Lee, Patrick McLeavey, Clive Streeter
Home Economists: Sue Ashworth, Jennie Berresford, Joanna Craig, Jill Eggleton,
Nicola Fowler, Carole Handslip, Jane Hartshorn, Kathryn Hawkins, Cara Hobday,
Deh-ta Hsiung, Wendy Lee, Louise Steele, Rosemary Wadey, Pamela Westland

The publishers would like to thank the British Chicken Information Service for providing
the recipes on pages 22, 39, 55–61, 74–75, 80–88, 90–91, 115–119, 131–134, 140–147, 153–157,
166–167, 182–194, 195, 207–216.

Recipes on the following pages courtesy of Tom Bridge: 23–24, 26–30, 32–35,
62–68, 72–73, 76–79, 89, 106–113, 130, 135–139, 158–161, 217–219

The publishers would like to thank Divertimenti for kindly loaning them equipment
for the following pages: 60, 73, 75, 80, 83, 91, 112, 116, 117, 130, 143, 144, 154, 189, 191, 192, 193, 211

Note
Tablespoons are assumed to be 15 ml. Unless otherwise stated, milk is assumed to be
full-fat, eggs are medium and pepper is freshly ground black pepper.

Contents

Roasts & Bakes 70

Casseroles 92

Quick Chicken Dishes 120

Introduction

Chicken has become justly popular around the whole world and plays an important part in the modern diet, being reasonably priced and nutritionally sound. It was not always the case, at one time only the affluent could afford to eat chicken. It was not until after World War II, when modern production methods started, that chicken became more plentiful and cheaper, enabling everyone to take advantage of a low-cost, healthy food.

Chicken is a versatile meat that lends itself to an enormous range of recipes, cooking methods and cuisines. Its unassertive flavour means that it is equally suited to cooking with herbs, spices, fruit, vegetables, and sweet and savoury flavours. Because it has a low fat content, especially without the skin, it is an ideal meat for low cholesterol and calorie-controlled diets – 105 grams/3½ ounces of white meat contains only 4 grams of fat. If you want to reduce fat further, cooking methods that require little added fat include poaching, grilling, roasting, or stir-frying. The skin can be left on during cooking to keep the meat moist and then removed before serving to reduce the fat content. As well as being an excellent source of protein, chicken contains valuable minerals, such as potassium and phosphorus, and some of the B vitamins.

There are many different types of chicken available. Whole birds come as broilers or roasters, boilers, which are older birds that need longer cooking, and small baby chickens, known as poussins. Broilers are also sold jointed into portions. Further options to choose from concern feeding and rearing methods. These include corn or maize-fed chickens, free-range chickens that are not reared intensively but are free to roam in a traditional farmyard and Poulet de Bresse, a French breed that is larger than normal.

The recipes in this book encompass several cooking methods and are gathered from many different cuisines. Choose from soups, starters, snacks and salads, roasts and bakes, casseroles, quick chicken dishes, pies, pastries and terrines, barbecues and grills, and hot and spicy dishes. As well as all the classic dishes, there are creative, contemporary recipes with some surprising twists. Whatever the occasion, the perfect dish is guaranteed to be found in this book.

Buying Guide

When buying fresh chicken, always check the sell-by date and make sure that the chicken feels chilled. Look for chicken that is undamaged, with no dark patches and few traces of feathers. Check the smell, which should be clean and fresh. Remove any giblets and store these separately. The flesh should feel soft and flexible and give slightly when pressed.

CHOOSING A CHICKEN

Baby chicken Also known as poussin or Cornish game hen, these are 4–6-week old birds weighing between 350–625 grams/12–20 ounces. One whole bird is usually needed for each person. Because they are so young and have not developed a lot of flavour, flavour must be added in the form of stuffing or a marinade.

Boiling fowl These are large birds over 10 months old, with a good flavour. They are ideal for casseroles or for making stock, but are generally too tough for roasting or grilling.

Broiler or frying chicken These birds are reared to produce tender flesh, and are usually 6–8 weeks old, weighing 1.5–2 kg/3–4lb. They are best used jointed and grilled or fried, but whole birds can also be roasted, steamed or casseroled.

Capon These are large, castrated cockerels, about 10 weeks old, and can weigh as much as 5 kg/10 lb. They have a greater proportion of white meat and the flesh is delicately marbled with fat which gives it an excellent flavour. In the UK, it is illegal to produce capons.

Corn-fed chicken These are reared on a diet containing large amounts of corn, a food often used in south-west France. The corn is thought to give a good flavour and the skin of these birds is a distinctive yellow colour. They usually weigh between 1.5–2.25 kg/ 3–5 lb.

Free-range chicken These have the freedom to feed at will and the space to run free, either in large, airy barns or in the farmyard. Barn-reared birds are slaughtered at 8–10 weeks, and farmyard birds at 1–12 weeks. They have a bigger, broader shape than the factory-reared broiler or roaster, and usually have a better flavour.

Poulet de Bresse Reared in the Burgundy region of France, these birds are fed on natural, high-quality food in free-range conditions. Perhaps because of this, their flavour is believed to be superior and this is reflected in their price.

Roaster These weigh about 1.8–3.5 kg/4–8 lb and are about 10 weeks old when slaughtered. They are best roasted whole, but if they are not too large, they can be jointed and used for frying or grilling.

Spring chicken Also known as a double poussin, this is a 9–12-week-old bird, weighing about 1.25 kg/2½ lb, which is large enough to feed two people.

Chicken Cuts

When you do not require a whole chicken, various choices of chicken cuts are available ready-packaged. Using cuts means quicker cooking and no wastage. There are choices of preparation as some chicken pieces are skinless and boneless while others have both bone and skin. Of course, the more preparation that is done, the more expensive the cut will be.

Breast
Chicken breasts are available with or without skin and either boneless or with the bone left in. The white meat is lean and succulent and can be simply cooked in butter or oil, or stuffed to add extra flavour.

Leg
The leg can be easily separated into a drumstick and thigh. If left as one piece, a large cut such as this is best poached or casseroled rather than grilled or fried.

Drumstick
This cut is convenient to eat at barbecues or buffet meals as it can be picked up easily. It is ideal for frying or barbecuing and can be first marinated or coated in breadcrumbs.

Thigh
Any slow-cooking method is suitable for this cut, and it is good used in recipes for casseroles and stews. The meat on thighs is dark but it is very succulent and juicy.

Wing
Although not very meaty, many people enjoy this cut when fried or roasted. If the wing tips are cut off, wings are a good candidate for the barbecue.

Minced chicken
Where a mild flavour is preferred, minced chicken makes a good substitute for minced red meat. It is also useful to make patties, rissoles and sausages.

Chicken liver
This is found either in the freezer or delicatessen. It is very tasty in rice dishes and can be used to make pâtés or cooked and tossed over warm salads.

Preparation Techniques

There are a number of different ways of preparing a whole chicken for cooking. The following techniques will help to make carving easier, speed up cooking times and even help to save you some money!

Spatchcocking

The spatchcocking technique involves flattening the bird so that it can be cooked more quickly. This method is ideal for grilling or barbecuing.

1 Put the chicken on a chopping board with the breast downwards. Cut through the bottom part of the carcass using poultry shears or heavy kitchen scissors, making sure not to cut right through to the breast bone below.

2 Rinse the chicken with cold water, drain and place on a board with the skin side uppermost. Press the chicken flat, then cut off the leg ends. Thread two long wooden skewers through the bird to keep it flat.

Jointing a Chicken

Jointing a chicken yourself is a cheaper option than buying ready-prepared portions and you can choose whether to cut the chicken into four or eight portions. Use either poultry shears or a sharp knife and strong kitchen scissors. First remove the legs: use a sharp knife and cut through the skin where the leg is attached to the body. Hold the leg away from the body and twist to break the ball and socket joint. Cut through the joint and remove the leg. Remove the other leg in the same way. Separate the breast from the back-bone, cut through the flap of skin below the rib cage and cut towards the neck. Pull the breast and back apart and cut through the joints that connect them. Take one side of the breast in each hand and hold skin side down. Bend each side until the breastbone becomes free. Remove it with your fingers and a knife. Cut the breast in half through the wishbone. Now cut each breast in half so that some is included with each wing. Finally, separate the thigh and drumstick.

Boning a Chicken

To make carving simpler, it is necessary to bone a chicken. Use a sharp knife with a short blade and keep the knife against the bone, using short, scraping actions.

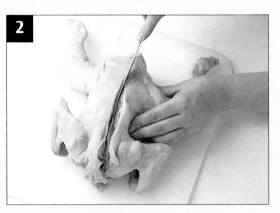

1 Dislocate each leg by breaking it at the thigh joint. Carefully remove the wishbone with the small knife.

2 With the bird breast-side down on a chopping board, cut down the centre of the backbone from the neck to the tail end.

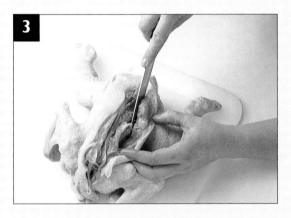

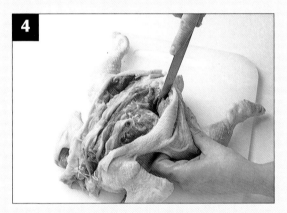

3 Working from the front to the back, scrape away the flesh on one side of the backbone, cutting into the bird to expose the ribcage.

4 Repeat on the other side, being careful not to pierce the breast skin with the knife. Pull the rib and backbone from the flesh of the bird.

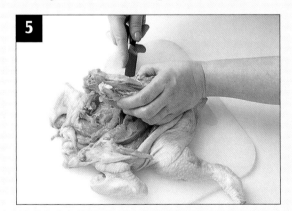

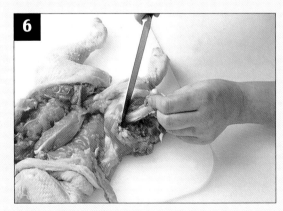

5 Scrape away the flesh from each thigh bone and cut away the bone at the joint with the small knife or poultry shears. Scrape all the flesh away from the wings up to the first joint.

6 Remove the exposed wing bone by cutting away the rest of the wing at the joint. Cut away the tendon from each fillet and breast. The chicken is now ready for stuffing and rolling.

Cooking Methods for Chicken

All types of chicken can be roasted, from baby chickens to larger birds.
With crisp, golden-brown skin and moist, succulent meat,
a perfectly roasted chicken is always popular.

ROASTING

Before roasting, remove any fat from the body cavity. Rinse the bird inside and out with water, then pat dry with paper towels. Season the cavity generously with salt and pepper and add stuffing, herbs or lemon if wished. Spread the breast of the chicken with softened butter or oil. Set on a rack in a roasting tin or shallow baking dish. Roast the bird, and baste two or three times with the pan juices during roasting.

Alternatively, cover the chicken with a piece of muslin that has been dipped in melted butter and there is no need to baste. If the chicken is browning too quickly, cover it with foil. Test for doneness by using a meat thermometer or insert a skewer into the thickest part of the thigh. If the chicken is cooked, the juices will run clear with no trace of pink. Put the bird on a carving board and leave to rest for at least 15 minutes before serving. Make a sauce or gravy from the juices left in the roasting tin.

Carving a Chicken

1 Grasp the leg and move it outwards from the body. Using a sharp knife, cut each drumstick and thigh from the body then cut through the joint to separate the drumstick and thigh.

2 Make a deep horizontal cut just above the wing, through the breast, until the knife touches the breastbone.

3 Slice the breast thinly in a series of vertical cuts going down to the first horizontal cut.

CHICKEN ROASTING TIMES

Type of chicken & temperature	Weight	Cooking time
Poussin 180°C/350°F/Gas Mark 4	500–750 g/1–1½ lb	1–1¼ hours
Chicken 190°C/375°F/Gas Mark 5	1.25–1.5 kg/2½ –3 lb	1–1¼ hours
	1.75–2 kg/3½–4 lb	1¼–2 hours
	2.25–2.5 kg/4½–5 lb	1½ –2 hours
	2.5–3 kg/5–6 lb	1¾–2¼ hours

Grilling

Grilling is a good way of cooking chicken. The intense heat of the grill quickly seals the succulent flesh beneath a crisp, golden exterior. For the best results the chicken should be placed 10–15 cm/4–6 inches away from a moderate heat source. If the chicken seems to be browning too quickly, turn down the heat slightly. If the chicken is grilled at too high a temperature too near to the heat, the outside will burn before the inside is cooked. If it is cooked for too long under a low heat, it will dry out. Baby chickens, spring chickens and small roasters are least likely to dry out and become tough. So that it can brown and cook evenly, cut a whole chicken into joints. For small chickens, split the chicken on either side of the backbone and cut the backbone out, then with the bird breast-side up, press firmly on the breastbone to break it and flatten the breast. Fold the wing tips back and behind and thread a long metal skewer through one wing, then the breast and out through the other wing. Thread another skewer through the thighs. This technique is known as spatchcocking. Chicken quarters are best reduced to smaller cuts. Divide leg portions into thighs and drumsticks. Breast meat, if cooked in one piece, can be rather dry and is best divided into bite-sized chunks for kebabs, or sliced and pounded flat to make escalopes. Wings are perfect for speedy grilling – the bones disperse the heat and the skin traps moisture to make a wonderfully succulent, tasty dish.

GRILLING TIMES FOR CHICKEN	
TYPE OF CHICKEN	COOKING TIME
Chicken portions	30–35 minutes
Skinless, boneless chicken breast	10–12 minutes
Spring chicken, spatchcocked	25–30 minutes
Poussin, spatchcocked	20–25 minutes
Roasting chicken, halved or spatchcocked	30–40 minutes

Marinades

- Chicken in Pitta Bread *(see page 51)*
- Supreme of Chicken with Black Cherries *(see page 76)*
- Chicken in Spicy Yogurt *(see page 171)*
- Jerk Chicken *(see page 176)*
- Thai Chicken with Peanut Sauce *(see page 178)*
- Sweet and Sour Drumsticks *(see page 195)*

FRYING

This cooking method is suitable for small thighs, drumsticks and joints. To pan-fry, first dry the chicken pieces with kitchen paper so that they brown properly and to prevent spitting during cooking. If required, the chicken can be coated in seasoned flour, egg and breadcrumbs or a batter. Heat oil or a mixture of oil and butter in a heavy frying pan. When the oil is very hot, add the chicken pieces, skin-side down. Fry until deep golden brown all over, turning the pieces frequently during cooking. The breast usually cooks before the drumsticks and thighs. Drain well on kitchen paper before serving.

SAUTEEING

This method is ideal for small pieces or small birds such as baby chickens. It can combine braising, where the chicken is first sautéed then cooked in stock or other liquid. Heat a little oil or a mixture of oil and butter in a heavy frying pan. Add the chicken and fry over a moderate heat until golden brown, turning often during cooking to brown all over. Add stock or other liquid, bring to the boil, then cover and reduce the heat. Cook gently until the chicken is cooked through.

STIR-FRYING

Skinless, boneless chicken is cut into pieces of equal size, either strips, small cubes or thin slices. This ensures that the meat cooks evenly and stays succulent. Preheat a wok or saucepan before adding a small amount of oil. When the oil starts to smoke, add the chicken pieces and stir-fry with your chosen flavourings for 3–4 minutes until cooked through. Other ingredients can be cooked at the same time, or the chicken can be cooked by itself, then removed from the pan while you stir-fry the remaining ingredients. Return the chicken to the pan briefly when the other ingredients are cooked.

CASSEROLING

Casseroling is a method that is good for cooking joints from larger, more mature chickens, although smaller chickens can be cooked whole. The slow cooking produces tender meat with a good flavour. Brown the chicken in butter or hot oil or a mixture of both. Add some stock, wine or a mixture of both with seasonings and herbs, cover and cook on top of the stove or in the oven until the chicken is tender. Add a selection of lightly sautéed vegetables about halfway through the cooking time.

BRAISING

This method does not require liquid – the chicken pieces or a small whole chicken and vegetables are cooked together slowly in a low oven. Heat some oil in an ovenproof, flameproof casserole and gently fry the chicken until golden all over. Remove the chicken and fry a selection of vegetables until they are almost tender. Replace the chicken, cover tightly and cook very gently on the top of the stove or in a low oven until the chicken and vegetables are tender.

POACHING

Poaching is a gentle cooking method that produces tender chicken and a stock that can be used to make a sauce to serve with the chicken. Put a whole chicken, a bouquet garni, a leek, a carrot and an onion in a large flameproof casserole. Cover with water, season and bring to the boil. Cover and simmer for $1\frac{1}{2}$–2 hours until the chicken is tender. Lift the chicken out, discard the bouquet garni and use the stock to make a sauce. The vegetables can be blended to thicken the stock and served with the chicken.

Food Safety & Tips

Chicken is liable to be contaminated by salmonella bacteria, which can cause severe food poisoning. When storing, handling and preparing poultry, certain precautions must be observed to prevent the possibility of food poisoning.

- Check the sell-by date and best before date. After buying, take the chicken home quickly, preferably in a freezer bag or cool box.

- Return frozen birds immediately to the freezer.

- If storing in the refrigerator, remove the wrappings and store any giblets separately. Place the chicken in a shallow dish to catch drips. Cover loosely with foil and store on the bottom shelf of the refrigerator for no more than two or three days, depending on the best before date. Avoid any contact between raw chicken and cooked food during storage and preparation. Wash your hands after handling raw chicken.

- Prepare raw chicken on a chopping board that can be easily cleaned and bleached, such as a non-porous, plastic board.

- Check the temperature of the refrigerator regularly, it should not exceed 4°C/42°F.

- Frozen birds should be defrosted before cooking. If time permits, defrost for about 36 hours in the refrigerator, or thaw for about 12 hours in a cool place. Bacteria breed in warm food at room temperature and when chicken is thawing. Cooking at high temperatures kills bacteria. There should be no ice crystals and the flesh should feel soft and flexible. Cook as soon as possible after thawing.

- Make sure that chicken is thoroughly cooked. Test for doneness using a meat thermometer – the thigh should reach at least 79°C/175°F when cooked – or pierce the thickest part of a thigh with a skewer, the juices should run clear, not pink or red. Never partially cook chicken with the intention of completing cooking later. Bacteria multiply at an alarming rate, particularly in warm food or during thawing, when optimum conditions prevail for the bacteria to increase.

Chicken Stock

Chicken stock is usually made from a whole bird or wings, backs and legs. This makes a well-flavoured stock. However it can also be made using chicken bones and carcass cooked with vegetables and flavourings. Although it will not be so rich in flavour it is still superior to stock made from a stock cube. Home-made stock can be stored in the freezer for up to six months. A simple chicken stock can be made using the giblets (except the liver which is bitter) with a bouquet garni, onion, carrot and some peppercorns. Salt is not added as this concentrates in flavour as the stock reduces during cooking. Salt can be added to taste when the stock is used in soups and other dishes.

If a whole bird is used to make the stock, the meat can be used in soups and casseroles.

To make chicken stock: Add the wings, backs or whole chicken to a large stockpot with two quartered onions. Cook until the chicken and onion are evenly browned. Cover with cold water, bring to the boil and skim off any scum that rises to the surface. Add two chopped carrots, two chopped celery sticks, a small bunch of parsley, a few bay leaves, a thyme sprig and a few peppercorns. Partially cover and gently simmer for about 3 hours. Strain the stock into a bowl and cool, then chill. When the stock is completely cold, remove the fat that will have set on the surface.

Stuffings for Chicken

- **Springtime Roast Chicken**
  (see page 80)
- **Pollo Catalan** *(see page 82)*
- **Festive Apple Chicken** *(see page 85)*
- **Golden Chicken with Mango &
  Cranberries** *(see page 90)*

Tips for Reducing Fat without Losing Flavour

- Roast whole chickens with their skin, but remove the skin before serving.

- Use cooking methods that don't require added fat, such as steaming, grilling, stir-frying, baking and roasting.

Stir-frying: Use just a little oil – once it is hot, it spreads further.

Poaching: Poach chicken in stock with added chopped vegetables. When the chicken is cooked through, purée the vegetables and stock to make a tasty sauce.

Baking: Dip chicken pieces in egg white, then into rolled oats or wholemeal flour before baking *(see page 57)*.

Steaming: Steam chicken over a smoky flavoured tea, such as lapsang souchong.

Grilling: Flavour can be added by first marinating the chicken. On the grill, fat drips away.

- Make gravy with the meat juices, after skimming off the fat. Add chicken stock and fresh herbs for flavour.

- Remove the skin from chicken pieces and rub a mixture of crushed garlic, chopped fresh herbs and spices over the chicken before cooking *(see page 72)*.

- Use marinades such as lemon or lime juice, wine and vinegar to add fat-free flavour.

- Add chopped onion or shallots, either sprinkled over chicken pieces, or placed inside a whole chicken.

- Spread skinless whole chicken or chicken pieces with mustard, or a mixture of honey and mustard with a squeeze of lime juice.

- Serve simply grilled chicken with fruit or vegetable salsas *(see page 61)*.

Soups

Chicken soup has a long tradition of being comforting and good for us and some cultures even think of it as a cure for all ills. It is certainly satisfying, full of flavour and easy to digest. For the best results, choose a boiling fowl or a large roasting bird, because immature birds sold for frying are not flavourful enough to make a tasty soup. Most chicken soups benefit from

being made from a good homemade chicken stock, although when time is at a premium, a good quality stock cube can be used instead. Every cuisine in the world has its own favourite version of chicken soup and in this section you'll find a selection of recipes from as far afield as Italy, Scotland and China. The recipes are easy to make and will inspire to you make your own variation of this delicious soup.

Thai Chicken Noodle Soup

Quick to make, this hot and spicy soup is hearty and warming. If you like your food really fiery, add a chopped dried or fresh chilli with its seeds.

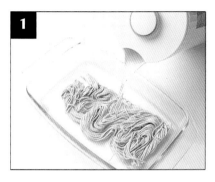

3 Add the drained noodles and heat through. Spoon into bowls and serve with a spoon and fork.

COOK'S VARIATION

Green Thai curry paste can be used instead of red curry paste for a less fiery flavour.

Serves 4–6
1 sheet of dried egg noodles from a 280 g/9 oz pack
1 tbsp oil
4 skinless, boneless chicken thighs, diced
1 bunch spring onions, sliced
2 garlic cloves, chopped
2 cm/$^3/_4$ in piece fresh ginger root, finely chopped
900 ml/1$^1/_2$ pints chicken stock
200 ml/7 fl oz coconut milk
3 tsp red Thai curry paste
3 tbsp peanut butter
2 tbsp light soy sauce
1 small red pepper, chopped
60 g/2 oz frozen peas
salt and pepper

1 Put the noodles in a shallow dish and soak in boiling water as the pack directs.

2 Heat the oil in a large saucepan or wok, add the chicken, and fry for 5 minutes, stirring until lightly browned. Add the white part of the spring onions, the garlic and ginger and fry for 2 minutes, stirring. Add the stock, coconut milk, curry paste, peanut butter and soy sauce. Season. Bring to the boil, stirring, then simmer for 8 minutes, stirring occasionally. Add the red pepper, peas and green spring onion tops and cook for 2 minutes.

Chicken Consommé

This is a very flavourful soup, especially if you make it from real chicken stock.
Egg shells are used to give a crystal clear appearance.

Serves 8–10
1.75 litres/3 pints chicken stock
150 ml/¼ pint medium sherry
4 egg whites plus egg shells
125 g/4 oz cooked chicken, sliced thinly
salt and pepper

1 Place the chicken stock and sherry in a large saucepan and heat gently for 5 minutes.

2 Add the egg whites and the egg shells to the chicken stock and whisk until the mixture begins to boil.

3 When the mixture boils, remove the pan from the heat and allow the mixture to subside for 10 minutes. Repeat this process three times.

4 This allows the egg white to trap the sediments in the chicken stock to clarify the soup.

5 Let the consommé cool for 5 minutes.

6 Carefully place a piece of fine muslin over a clean saucepan. Ladle the soup over the muslin and strain into the saucepan.

7 Repeat this process twice, then gently re-heat the consommé. Season to taste, add the chicken slices to the consommé and serve.

Cream of Chicken Soup

Tarragon adds a delicate aniseed flavour to this tasty soup.
If you can't find tarragon, use parsley for a fresh taste.

Serves 4

60g/2 oz unsalted butter
1 large onion, peeled and chopped
300 g/10 oz cooked chicken,
shredded finely
600 ml/1 pint chicken stock
1 tbsp chopped fresh tarragon
150ml/1/4 pint double cream
salt and pepper
fresh tarragon leaves, to garnish

1 Melt the butter in a large saucepan and fry the onion for 3 minutes.

2 Add the cooked chicken to the pan with 300 ml/1/2 pint of the chicken stock.

3 Bring the soup to the boil and simmer for 20 minutes. Allow to cool, then liquidize the soup.

4 Add the remainder of the stock and season with salt and pepper.

5 Add the chopped tarragon, pour the soup into a tureen and add a swirl of cream. Garnish with fresh tarragon and serve with deep fried croûtons.

COOK'S VARIATION

If you can't find fresh tarragon, freeze-dried tarragon makes a good substitute. Single cream can be used instead of the double cream.

Chicken Wonton Soup

This Chinese-style soup is delicious as a starter
to an oriental meal or as a light meal.

4 Cook the filled wontons in boiling water for 1 minute or until they float to the top.

5 Remove with a slotted spoon. Bring the chicken stock to the boil.

6 Add the soy sauce, spring onion and carrot. Add the wontons to the soup and simmer gently for 2 minutes. Serve at once.

Serves 4–6

FILLING

350 g/12 oz minced chicken

1 tbsp soy sauce

1 tsp grated, fresh ginger root

1 garlic clove, crushed

2 tsp sherry

2 spring onions, chopped

1 tsp sesame oil

1 egg white

$^1/_2$ tsp cornflour

$^1/_2$ tsp sugar

about 35 wonton wrappers

SOUP

1.5 litres/2$^1/_2$ pints chicken stock

1 tbsp light soy sauce

1 spring onion, shredded

1 small carrot, cut into very thin slices

1 Combine all the ingredients for the filling and mix well.

2 Place a small spoonful of the filling in the centre of each wonton wrapper.

3 Dampen the edges and gather up the wonton wrapper to form a small pouch enclosing the filling.

COOK'S TIP

Look for wonton wrappers in Chinese or oriental supermarkets. Fresh wrappers can be found in the chilled compartment and they can be frozen if you wish. Wrap in clingfilm before freezing.

Dickensian Chicken Broth

This soup is made with traditional Scottish ingredients.
It should be left for at least two days before being re-heated,
then served with oatmeal cakes or bread.

Serves 4

60 g/2 oz
pre-soaked dried peas

900 g/2 lb diced chicken,
fat removed

1.2 litres/2 pints chicken stock

600ml/1 pint water

60 g/2 oz barley

1 large carrot, peeled and diced

1 small turnip, peeled and diced

1 large leek, thinly sliced

1 red onion, chopped finely

salt and white pepper

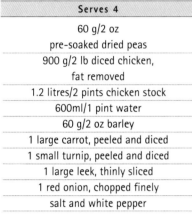

1 Put the peas and chicken into a pan, add the stock and water and bring slowly to the boil.

2 Skim the stock as it boils.

3 When all the scum is removed add the washed barley and salt and simmer for 35 minutes.

4 Add the rest of the ingredients and simmer for 2 hours.

5 Skim and allow the broth to stand for at least 24 hours. Reheat, adjust the seasoning and serve.

COOK'S TIP

Use either whole grain barley or pearl barley. Only the outer husk is removed from whole grain barley and when cooked it has a nutty flavour and a chewy texture.

Tom's Chicken Soup

The potato has been part of the Irish diet for centuries.
This recipe is originally from the north of Ireland, in the
beautiful area of Moira, County Down.

Serves 4
3 smoked, streaky, rindless bacon slices, chopped
500 g/1 lb boneless chicken, chopped
30 g/1 oz butter
3 medium potatoes, chopped
3 medium onions, chopped
600 ml/1 pint giblet or chicken stock
600 ml/1 pint cups milk
150 ml/¼ pint double cream
salt and pepper
2 tbsp chopped fresh parsley, to garnish

1 Gently fry the bacon and chicken in a large saucepan for 10 minutes.

2 Add the butter, potatoes and onions and cook for 15 minutes, stirring all the time.

3 Add the stock and milk, then bring the soup to the boil and simmer for 45 minutes. Season to taste.

4 Blend in the cream and simmer for 5 minutes, garnish with parsley and serve with Irish soda bread.

COOK'S TIP

Soda bread is not made with yeast as bread usually is. Instead it is made with bicarbonate of soda as the raising agent. It can be made with plain flour or wholemeal flour.

Chicken & Pea Soup

A hearty soup that is so simple to make yet packed with flavour.
You can use either whole green peas or green or yellow split peas.

Serves 4–6
3 smoked, streaky, rindless bacon slices, chopped
900 g/2 lb chicken, chopped
1 large onion, chopped
15 g/½ oz butter
500 g/1 lb ready-soaked peas
2.4 litres/4 pints chicken stock
150ml/¼ pint/⅔ cup double cream
2 tbsp chopped fresh parsley
salt and pepper
cheesy croûtes, to garnish

1 Put the bacon, chicken and onion into a large saucepan with a little butter and cook over a gentle heat for 8 minutes.

2 Add the peas and the stock to the pan, bring to the boil, season lightly with salt and pepper, cover and simmer for 2 hours.

3 Blend the cream into the soup, sprinkle with parsley and top with cheesy croûtes.

COOK'S TIP

Croûtes are slices of French bread that are fried or baked, then they can be sprinkled with grated cheese and lightly toasted.

Cream of Chicken & Lemon Soup

A refreshing soup with the fresh flavours of lemon
and parsley is perfect on summer days.

Serves 4
60 g/2 oz butter
8 shallots, sliced thinly
2 medium carrots, sliced thinly
2 stalks celery, sliced thinly
280 g/9 oz skinless chicken breast meat, chopped finely
3 lemons
1.2 litres/2 pints chicken stock
150ml/¼ pint double cream
salt and pepper
sprigs of parsley and lemon slices, to garnish

1 Melt the butter in a large saucepan, add the vegetables and chicken and cook gently for 8 minutes.

2 Thinly pare the lemons and blanch the lemon rind in boiling water for 3 minutes.

3 Squeeze the juice from the lemons.

4 Add the lemon rind and freshly squeezed lemon juice to the pan with the chicken stock.

5 Bring slowly to the boil and simmer for 50 minutes. Cool the soup then blend in a food processor. Return the soup to the saucepan, reheat, season to taste and add the double cream. Do not boil at this stage or the soup will curdle.

6 Transfer the soup to a tureen or individual bowls. Serve, garnished with parsley and lemon slices.

Cream of Chicken & Tomato Soup

This soup is very good made wih fresh tomatoes,
but if you prefer, you can use canned tomatoes.

Serves 2
60 g/2 oz unsalted butter
1 large onion, chopped
500 g/1 lb chicken, shredded very finely
600 ml/1 pint chicken stock
6 medium tomatoes, chopped finely
pinch of bicarbonate of soda
1 tbsp caster sugar
150ml/1¼ pint double cream
salt and pepper
fresh basil leaves, to garnish

1 Melt the butter in a large saucepan and fry the onion and shredded chicken for 5 minutes.

2 Add 300 ml/½ pint chicken stock to the pan, with the tomatoes and bicarbonate of soda.

3 Bring the soup to the boil and simmer for 20 minutes.

4 Allow the soup to cool, then blend the soup in a food processor.

5 Add the remaining chicken stock, season with salt and pepper, then add the sugar.

6 Pour the soup into a tureen and add a swirl of cream. Serve with croûtons and garnish with fresh basil leaves.

Cock-a-Leekie Soup

A traditional Scottish soup in which a whole chicken is cooked with vegetables
to add extra flavour to the stock. Add some of the cooked chicken to
the soup and reserve the remainder for another meal.

Serves 4
1–1.5 kg/2–3 lb oven-ready chicken plus giblets, if available
1.75–2 litres/3–3½ pints chicken stock
1 onion, sliced thinly
4 leeks, sliced thinly
good pinch of ground allspice or ground coriander seeds
1 bouquet garni, (bay leaf, parsley and thyme sprigs, tied with string)
12 no-soak prunes, halved and pitted
salt and pepper
warm crusty bread, to serve

1 Put the chicken and giblets, if using, stock and onion in a large saucepan. Bring to the boil and remove any scum from the surface.

2 Add the leeks, allspice or coriander, bouquet garni and salt and pepper. Cover and simmer for 1½ hours until the chicken is falling off the bone.

3 Remove the chicken from the pan and skim any fat from the surface of the soup.

4 Chop some of the chicken flesh and return to the pan. Add the prunes, bring back to the boil and simmer, uncovered, for about 20 minutes.

5 Discard the bouquet garni, adjust the seasoning and serve.

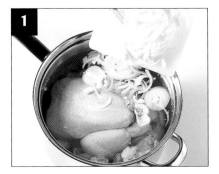

Chicken Mulligatawny Soup

This spicy soup was brought to the west by army
and service personnel returning from India.

Serves 4
60 g/2 oz butter
1 onion, sliced
1 garlic clove, crushed
500 g/1 lb chicken, diced
60 g/2 oz smoked rindless bacon, diced
1 small turnip, diced
2 carrots, diced
1 small cooking apple, diced
2 tbsp mild curry powder
1 tbsp curry paste
1 tbsp tomato purée
1 tbsp plain flour
1.2 litres/2 pints chicken stock
150ml/1/4 pint double cream
salt and pepper
1 tsp of chopped fresh coriander, to garnish

1 Melt the butter in a large saucepan and cook the onion, garlic, chicken and bacon for 5 minutes.

2 Add the turnip, carrots and apple and cook for a further two minutes.

3 Blend in the curry powder, curry paste and tomato purée, and sprinkle over the flour.

4 Add the chicken stock and bring to the boil, cover and simmer for 1 hour.

5 Liquidize the soup. Reheat, season to taste and gradually blend in the cream. Garnish with coriander and serve over small bowls of boiled or fried rice.

Cream of Chicken & Orange Soup

For a tangy flavour, lemons can be used instead of oranges and the recipe
can be adapted to make duck and orange soup.

Serves 4
60 g/2 oz butter
8 shallots, sliced thinly
2 medium carrots, sliced thinly
2 sticks celery, sliced thinly
250 g/8 oz skinless chicken breast, chopped finely
3 oranges
1.2 litres/2 pints chicken stock
150 ml/$\frac{1}{4}$ pint double cream
salt and white pepper
sprig of parsley and 3 orange slices, to garnish

1 Melt the butter in a large saucepan, add the vegetables and chicken meat and cook gently for 8 minutes.

2 Thinly pare the oranges and blanch the rind in boiling water for about 3 minutes.

3 Squeeze the juice from the oranges. Add the orange rind and freshly squeezed orange juice to the pan with the chicken stock.

4 Bring slowly to the boil and simmer for 50 minutes. Cool the soup then liquidize in a blender or food processor until smooth.

COOK'S VARIATION

Use 2 small lemons in place of the oranges. Look for organic or unwaxed lemons when using rind.

5 Return the soup to the saucepan, reheat, season to taste and add the cream. Do not boil at this stage or the soup will curdle.

6 Transfer the soup to a serving dish or individual bowls, and serve, garnished with a sprig of parsley, orange slices and soda bread.

Chicken Soup with Coriander Dumplings

Use the strained vegetables and chicken to make little patties. Simply mash with
a little butter, shape them into round cakes and fry in butter or oil until golden brown.

Serves 6–8
900 g/2 lb chicken meat, sliced
60 g/2 oz plain flour
125 g/4 oz butter
3 tbsp sunflower oil
1 large carrot, chopped
1 stick celery, chopped
1 onion, chopped
1 small turnip, chopped
120 ml/4 fl oz sherry
3 tbsp sunflower oil
1 tsp thyme
1 bay leaf
1.75 litres/3 pints chicken stock
salt and pepper
DUMPLINGS
60 g/2 oz self-raising flour
60 g/2 oz fresh breadcrumbs
2 tbsp shredded suet
2 tbsp chopped fresh coriander
2 tbsp finely grated lemon rind
1 egg
salt and pepper

1 Coat the chicken pieces lightly with the flour and season.

2 Melt the butter in a saucepan and fry the chicken pieces until they are lightly browned.

3 Add the oil to the pan and brown the vegetables together. Add the sherry with all the remaining ingredients except the chicken stock.

4 Cook for 10 minutes, then gradually add the chicken stock.

Simmer for three hours, skimming off any excess fat.

5 Strain the liquid into a large clean saucepan and allow to cool.

6 To make the dumplings, mix together all the dry ingredients in a large clean bowl.

7 Add the egg and blend in thoroughly then add enough milk to make a moist dough.

8 Shape the dough into small balls and roll them in a little flour.

9 Cook the dumplings in boiling salted water for 10 minutes.

10 Remove them carefully with a slotted spoon and add them to the soup. Cook for a further 12 minutes, then serve with crusty bread.

Chicken & Leek Soup

This satisfying soup can be served as a main course.
You can add rice and peppers to make it even more hearty, as well as colourful.

Serves 6
30 g/1 oz butter
350 g/12 oz boneless chicken
350 g/12 oz leeks, cut into 2.5-cm/1-inch pieces
1.2 litres/2 pints chicken stock
1 bouquet garni sachet
salt and white pepper
8 pitted prunes, halved
cooked rice and diced peppers

1 Melt the butter in a large saucepan, add the chicken and leeks and fry for 8 minutes.

2 Add the stock and bouquet garni sachet, and season well to taste.

3 Bring the soup to the boil and simmer for 45 minutes.

4 Add the prunes with some cooked rice and diced peppers if you wish, and simmer for 20 minutes. Remove the bouquet garni sachet and discard before serving.

COOK'S TIP

Instead of the bouquet garni sachet, you can use a bunch of fresh, mixed herbs, tied together with string. Choose herbs such as parsley, thyme and rosemary.

Chicken & Sweetcorn Soup

A hint of chilli and sherry flavour this chicken and sweetcorn soup,
which has both baby sweetcorn and corn niblets in it,
with red pepper and tomato for colour and flavour.

Serves 4

1 skinless, boneless chicken breast,
about 175 g/6 oz

2 tbsp sunflower oil

2–3 spring onions,
thinly sliced diagonally

1 small or ½ large red
pepper, thinly sliced

1 garlic clove, crushed

125 g/4 oz baby sweetcorn, thinly sliced

1 litre/1¾ pints chicken stock

200 g/7 oz can of sweetcorn
niblets, well drained

2 tbsp sherry

2–3 tsp bottled sweet
chilli sauce

2–3 tsp cornflour

2 tomatoes, quartered
and deseeded, then sliced

salt and pepper

chopped fresh coriander
or parsley, to garnish

1 Cut the chicken breast into 4 strips
lengthways, then cut each strip into
narrow slices across the grain.

2 Heat the oil in a wok or frying pan,
swirling it around until it is really hot.
Add the chicken and stir-fry for 3–4
minutes, moving it around the wok
until it is well sealed all over and
almost cooked through.

3 Add the spring onions, pepper and
garlic, and stir-fry for 2–3 minutes.
Add the sweetcorn and stock and
bring to the boil.

4 Add the sweetcorn niblets, sherry,

sweet chilli sauce and salt to taste,
and simmer for 5 minutes, stirring
from time to time.

5 Blend the cornflour with a little
cold water. Add to the soup and bring
to the boil, stirring until the sauce is

thickened. Add the tomato slices,
season to taste and simmer for 1–2
minutes. Serve the soup hot,
sprinkled with chopped coriander
or parsley.

Chicken Soup with Almonds

This soup can also be made using turkey or pheasant breasts.
Pheasant gives a stronger flavour, particularly if game stock
is made from the carcass and used in the soup.

Serves 4

1 large or 2 small skinless,
boneless chicken breasts

1 tbsp sunflower oil

1 carrot, cut into
julienne strips

4 spring onions, thinly sliced diagonally

700 ml/1¼ pints chicken stock

finely grated rind of ½ lemon

45 g/1½ oz ground almonds

1 tbsp light soy sauce

1 tbsp lemon juice

30 g/1 oz flaked almonds, toasted

salt and pepper

bread, to serve

1 Cut each breast into four strips
lengthways, then slice very thinly
across the grain into shreds.

2 Heat the oil in the wok, swirling it
around until really hot. Add the
chicken and toss it for 3–4 minutes
until sealed and almost cooked
through. Add the carrot and cook for
2–3 minutes, stirring all the time. Add
the spring onions and stir.

3 Add the stock to the wok and bring
to the boil. Add the lemon rind,
ground almonds, soy sauce, lemon
juice and plenty of salt and pepper.

4 Bring back to the boil and simmer,
uncovered, for 5 minutes, stirring.

5 Adjust the seasoning, add most of
the toasted flaked almonds and cook
for a further 1–2 minutes.

6 Serve the soup very hot, in
individual bowls, sprinkled with the
remaining almonds.

COOK'S VARIATION

If you prefer, use finely chopped,
skinless toasted hazelnuts in place of
the flaked almonds.

Vegetable & Chick-Pea Soup

A good tasty soup full of vegetables, chicken and chick-peas,
with just a hint of spiciness, to serve on any occasion.

Serves 4–6
3 tbsp olive oil
1 large onion, chopped finely
2–3 garlic cloves, crushed
1/2–1 red chilli, deseeded and chopped very finely
1 skinless, boneless chicken breast, about 150 g/5 oz, sliced thickly
2 celery sticks, chopped finely
175 g/6 oz carrots, grated coarsely
1.25 litres/2 1/4 pints chicken stock
2 bay leaves
1/2 tsp dried oregano
1/4 tsp ground cinnamon
425 g/14 oz can of chick-peas, drained
2 medium tomatoes, peeled, deseeded and chopped
1 tbsp tomato purée
salt and pepper
chopped fresh coriander or parsley, to garnish
corn or wheat tortillas, to serve

1 Heat the oil in a large saucepan and fry the onion, garlic and chilli very gently until they are softened but not coloured.

2 Add the chicken to the saucepan and continue to cook until well sealed and lightly browned.

3 Add the celery, carrots, stock, bay leaves, oregano, cinnamon, and salt and pepper. Bring to the boil, then cover and simmer gently for about 20 minutes, or until the chicken is tender and cooked throughout.

4 Remove the chicken from the soup and chop it finely, or cut it into narrow strips.

5 Return the chicken to the pan with the chick-peas, tomatoes and tomato purée. Simmer, covered, for a further

15–20 minutes. Discard the bay leaves, then adjust the seasoning.

6 Serve very hot sprinkled with coriander or parsley and accompanied by warmed tortillas.

Chicken & Pasta Broth

This satisfying soup makes a good lunch or supper dish and you can use any vegetables that you have at hand. Children will love the tiny pasta shapes.

Serves 4–6
350 g/12 oz boneless chicken breasts
2 tbsp sunflower oil
1 medium onion, diced
250 g/8 oz carrots, diced
250 g/8 oz cauliflower florets
900 ml/1$\frac{1}{2}$ pints chicken stock
2 tsp dried mixed herbs
125 g/4 oz small pasta shapes
salt and pepper
Parmesan cheese (optional) and crusty bread, to serve

1 Finely dice the chicken, discarding any skin.

2 Heat the oil and quickly sauté the chicken and vegetables until they are lightly coloured.

3 Stir in the stock and herbs. Bring to the boil and add the pasta. Return to the boil, cover and simmer for 10 minutes. Season to taste and sprinkle with Parmesan cheese, if using. Serve with crusty bread.

COOK'S VARIATION

Broccoli florets can be used to replace the cauliflower florets. Substitute 2 tablespoons chopped fresh mixed herbs for the dried mixed herbs.

Chicken & Sweetcorn Chowder

A quick and satisfying soup, full of flavour and different textures.
Sweetcorn is a sweet, juicy addition.

Serves 2
2 tsp oil
15 g/$\frac{1}{2}$ oz butter or margarine
1 small onion, chopped finely
1 chicken leg, quarter
or 2–3 drumsticks
1 tbsp plain flour
600 ml/1 pint chicken stock
$\frac{1}{2}$ small red, yellow
or orange pepper,
chopped finely
2 large tomatoes,
peeled and chopped
2 tsp tomato purée
200 g/7 oz can of sweetcorn, drained
generous pinch of dried oregano
$\frac{1}{4}$ tsp ground coriander seeds
salt and pepper
chopped fresh parsley,
to garnish

1 Heat the oil and butter or margarine in a saucepan and fry the onion gently until just beginning to soften. Cut the chicken quarter, if using, into two pieces. Add the chicken to the saucepan and fry until golden brown all over.

2 Add the flour and cook for 1–2 minutes. Then add the stock gradually, bring to the boil and simmer for about 5 minutes.

3 Add the pepper, tomatoes, tomato purée, sweetcorn, oregano, coriander, and salt and pepper. Cover and simmer gently for about 20 minutes until the chicken is very tender.

4 Remove the chicken from the soup, strip the flesh from the bone and chop it finely with a sharp knife. Then return the chicken to the soup.

5 Adjust the seasoning and simmer for a further 2–3 minutes before sprinkling with chopped, fresh parsley. Serve the soup very hot with crusty bread.

Noodles in Soup

Noodles in soup are popular in China. This is a thick, hearty soup, just add more stock if you prefer a thinner soup.

Serves 4
250 g/8 oz cooked, skinless, boneless chicken
3–4 Chinese dried mushrooms, soaked
125 g/4 oz can of sliced bamboo shoots, rinsed and drained
125 g/4 oz spinach, lettuce hearts, or Chinese leaves, shredded
2 spring onions, finely shredded
250 g/8 oz egg noodles
about 600 ml/1 pint chicken stock
2 tbsp light soy sauce
2 tbsp vegetable oil
1 tsp salt
1/2 tsp sugar
2 tsp Chinese rice wine or dry sherry
a few drops of sesame oil
1 tsp red chilli oil (optional)

1 Cut the meat into thin shreds. Squeeze dry the soaked mushrooms and discard the hard stalk.

2 Thinly shred the mushrooms, bamboo shoots, spinach and spring onions.

3 Cook the noodles in boiling water according to the instructions on the packet, then drain and rinse under cold water. Place the noodles in a bowl and set aside. Bring the stock to a boil, add about 1 tablespoon soy sauce and pour over the noodles. Keep warm.

4 Heat the oil in a preheated wok or heavy frying pan, add about half of the spring onions, the chicken and the vegetables (mushrooms, bamboo shoots and greens). Stir-fry for about 2–3 minutes. Add all the seasonings and blend together well.

5 Pour the mixture into the wok over the noodles, garnish with the remaining spring onions and serve immediately.

Hot & Sour Soup

This is one of the most popular soups in Chinese
restaurants throughout the world.

Serves 4
4–6 dried oriental mushrooms (shiitake), soaked
125 g/4 oz cooked chicken or pork
1 cake tofu
60 g/2 oz can of sliced bamboo shoots, drained
1 tbsp cornflour
600 ml/1 pint chicken stock or water
1 tbsp Chinese rice wine or dry sherry
1 tbsp light soy sauce
2 tbsp rice vinegar
$\frac{1}{2}$ tsp ground white pepper
salt
2–3 spring onions, thinly sliced, to garnish

1 Drain the mushrooms, squeeze dry and discard the hard stalks. Thinly slice the mushrooms.

2 Thinly slice the chicken, tofu and bamboo shoots into narrow shreds using a cleaver.

3 Mix the cornflour with 1½ tablespoons of water to form a paste and set aside.

4 Bring the stock or water to a rolling boil in a wok or frying pan and add the mushrooms, chicken, tofu and bamboo shoots. Bring back to the boil then simmer for about 1 minute.

5 Add the wine, soy sauce and vinegar. Bring back to the boil, stirring in the cornflour paste. Add the pepper and season with salt to taste. Serve hot, sprinkled with the spring onions.

COOK'S TIP

Shiitake mushrooms have a pronounced flavour. Wipe the caps and stalks before cooking.

Chicken & Noodle One-Pot

Flavoursome chicken and vegetables cooked with Chinese egg noodles in a coconut sauce.
Increase the amount of stock for a thinner soup. Serve the soup in deep bowls.

Serves 4
1 tbsp sunflower oil
1 onion, sliced
1 garlic clove, crushed
2.5 cm/1 inch fresh ginger root, grated
1 bunch spring onions, sliced diagonally
500 g/1 lb skinless, boneless chicken breasts, cut into bite-sized pieces
2 tbsp mild curry paste
500 ml/16 fl oz coconut milk
300 ml/$\frac{1}{2}$ pint chicken stock
250 g/8 oz Chinese egg noodles
2 tsp lime juice
salt and pepper
sprigs of basil, to garnish

1 Heat the oil in a wok or large, heavy-based frying pan. Add the onion, garlic, ginger and spring onions and stir-fry for 2 minutes until softened.

2 Add the chicken pieces and curry paste. Stir-fry for about 4 minutes until the vegetables and chicken are golden brown.

3 Stir in the coconut milk, stock and salt and pepper to taste, mixing until well blended. Bring to the boil.

4 Add the noodles to the pan. Cover and simmer for about 6–8 minutes, stirring occasionally until the noodles are just tender.

5 Add the lime juice, season to taste and garnish with basil sprigs. Serve at once in deep soup bowls.

COOK'S TIP

Look for canned coconut milk in Asian and oriental supermarkets or in delicatessens.

Starters, Snacks & Salads

Chicken is versatile and quick to cook, making it perfect for innovative and appetizing first courses or light lunches. Its unassertive flavour means that it can be enlivened by exotic fruits and spices and oriental ingredients, such as mirin, sesame oil and fresh ginger root. It is infused with a spicy Middle Eastern flavour after marinating in a rich mixture of spices, then

served in pitta bread with salad and herbed yogurt. There are fritters, classic salads, rarebits, pâtés, potted chicken, fillings for baked potatoes, and drumsticks that are stuffed and baked, or served with delicious fruity salsas. Because chicken pieces travel well and are easy to eat, many of the recipes are ideal to take on picnics or to pack into a lunch box. The recipes are cosmopolitan, with influences appearing from as far apart as the Mediterranean and Asia.

Oriental Chicken Salad

Mirin, soy sauce and sesame oil give an oriental
flavour to this fresh-tasting salad.

Serves 4
750 g/1½ lb skinless chicken
75 ml/3 fl oz mirin or sweet sherry
75 ml/3 fl oz light soy sauce
1 tbsp sesame oil
3 tbsp olive oil
1 tbsp red wine vinegar
1 tbsp Dijon mustard
250 g/8 oz egg noodles
250 g/8 oz bean-sprouts
250 g/8 oz Chinese leaves, shredded
2 spring onions, sliced
125 g/4 oz mushrooms, sliced

5 Toss the bean-sprouts, Chinese leaves, spring onions and mushrooms with the noodles.

6 Slice the cooked chicken very thinly and stir into the noodles. Serve the salad immediately

1 Pound the chicken pieces out to an even thickness between two sheets of clingfilm with a rolling pin or cleaver.

2 Put the chicken in a roasting tin. Combine the mirin and soy sauce and brush the mixture over the chicken. Place in a preheated oven, 200°C/400°F/Gas Mark 6, for 20–30 minutes, basting often. Remove from the oven and allow to cool slightly.

3 Meanwhile, combine the sesame oil, olive oil and vinegar with the Dijon mustard.

4 Cook the noodles according to the packet instructions. Rinse under cold running water, then drain and immediately toss in the dressing.

Chicken, Papaya & Avocado Salad

Try this recipe with peaches or nectarines instead of papaya.

Serves 4
4 skinless, boneless chicken breasts
1 red chilli, deseeded and chopped
1¹/₂ tbsp red wine vinegar
75 ml/3fl oz olive oil
1 papaya, peeled
1 avocado, peeled
125 g/4 oz alfalfa sprouts
125 g/4 oz bean-sprouts
salt and pepper

1 Poach the chicken breasts in boiling water for 15 minutes or until cooked through. Remove with a slotted spoon and set aside to cool.

2 Combine the chilli, vinegar and oil, season well and set aside.

3 Thinly slice the chicken breasts with a sharp knife.

4 Slice the papaya and avocado to the same thickness as the chicken. Arrange on four plates with the alfalfa sprouts and bean-sprouts. Serve accompanied by the dressing.

COOK'S TIP

If you are using papaya rather than peaches in this recipe, add a little lime juice and grated lime rind to the chilli dressing, for an extra tangy flavour.

Chicken Pasta Provençale

Use any pasta shape for this salad, but drain thoroughly
so that it does not dilute the dressing.

Serves 4
175 g/6 oz dried pasta shapes
4 tbsp French Dressing (see below)
2 tbsp olive oil
350 g/12 oz skinless, boneless chicken breast, cut into strips
2 courgettes, sliced
1 red pepper, deseeded and cut into chunks
2 garlic cloves, sliced
4 tomatoes, cut into wedges
60 g/2 oz can of anchovies, drained and chopped
30 g/1 oz black olives, pitted and halved
sprig of fresh parsley, to garnish

FRENCH DRESSING

3 tbsp olive oil
1 tbsp wine vinegar
1 garlic clove, crushed
$^1/_2$ tsp Dijon or Meaux mustard
1 tsp clear honey
salt and pepper

1 Cook the pasta in boiling salted water for 10–12 minutes until 'al dente'. Drain thoroughly.

2 Whisk all the dressing ingredients together until thoroughly blended.

3 Put the pasta into a bowl with the dressing and mix together.

4 Heat the oil in a frying pan. Add the chicken and stir-fry for 4–5 minutes, stirring occasionally until cooked, then remove from the pan.

5 Add the courgettes, pepper and garlic to the pan. Fry for 12–15 minutes, stirring, until softened.

6 Add the tomatoes, anchovies and olives to the pasta with the chicken and fried vegetables,

and mix thoroughly together.

7 Transfer to a serving dish, garnish with parsley and serve immediately while warm.

Chicken Liver & Watercress Paté

The peppery flavours of the watercress really come through in this soft pâté – try serving
it on hot melba toast as a delicious snack

Serves 4–6
60g/2 oz butter
1 onion, chopped
250g/8 oz chicken livers
1 garlic clove, chopped
125g/4 oz watercress, trimmed and chopped
1 tbsp chopped fresh thyme
1 tbsp chopped fresh parsley
1 tbsp sherry
salt and pepper
sprig of watercress, to garnish

1 Heat the butter in a frying pan and fry the onion gently for about 5 minutes until soft.

2 Add the chicken livers and garlic and fry gently for 3–4 minutes until cooked through.

3 Set aside to cool slightly, before stirring in the watercress, fresh herbs and sherry.

4 Transfer the mixture to a food processor and process until the chicken livers are finely chopped, but still have some texture – alternatively, put the mixture through a food mill.

5 Transfer the mixture to a serving dish. Cover and leave in the refrigerator to chill. Serve on hot melba toast.

Potted Chicken

Cooked poultry, meat and game can all be prepared in this traditional way:
finely minced and cooked with onions, spices and sherry or port.
Serve as a first course or sandwich filling.

Serves 4–6

250 g/8 oz boneless
cooked chicken leg meat or any
boneless game, beef or lamb

125 g/4 oz butter

1 onion, chopped very finely

1–2 garlic cloves, crushed

2 tbsp sherry or port

about 4 tbsp stock

good pinch of ground mace,
nutmeg or allspice

pinch of dried mixed herbs

salt and pepper

sprigs of fresh thyme, to garnish

TO SERVE

sprigs of watercress

cherry tomatoes
or tomato wedges

crusty bread or fingers of toast

1 Remove any skin and gristle from the poultry, game or meat. Finely mince twice, or finely chop in a food processor.

2 Melt half the butter in a saucepan and fry the onion and garlic gently until soft but only lightly coloured.

3 Stir the chicken into the pan, followed by the sherry or port and just enough of the stock to moisten the mixture.

4 Season to taste with salt, pepper, mace and herbs. Press the mixture into a lightly greased dish or several small individual dishes and level the top. Cover and chill until firm.

5 Melt the remaining butter and pour a thin layer over the potted chicken. gently press in a few sprigs of thyme and chill thoroughly so that the herbs set in the butter.

6 Serve spooned on to plates, or in individual pots on plates, garnished with watercress, tomatoes and crusty bread or fingers of toast.

Chicken in Pitta Bread

Pitta bread makes a great container for fast and flavoursome meals – either on the move or for a weekend lunch.

Serves 4

1 tbsp cumin seed, crushed

1 tbsp coriander seed, crushed

1 tbsp ground turmeric

1 tbsp black mustard seed

2 tsp chilli flakes

50 ml/2 fl oz olive oil

750 g/1 1/2 lb skinless, boneless chicken thighs

300 ml/1/2 pt natural yogurt

90 g/3 oz fresh coriander

90 g/3 oz fresh mint

juice of 1 lime

salt and pepper

TO SERVE

4 pitta breads

salad leaves

cucumber slices

tomato wedges

baby tomatoes

sprig of fresh parsley, to garnish

1 Combine the cumin, coriander, turmeric, mustard seed, chilli flakes and oil. Season generously with salt and pepper.

2 Cut the chicken into finger width strips and place in a large bowl. Toss in the spice mixture. Leave to marinate for at least 2 hours, or as long as possible.

3 Cook the chicken in a preheated oven, 220°C/425°F/Gas Mark 7, for 15 minutes, turning once or twice.

4 Combine the yogurt and herbs in a food processor until smooth, or finely chop the herbs and stir into the yogurt. Add the lime juice and season well with salt and pepper.

5 To serve, split the pitta breads and warm them through. Stuff generously with salad leaves, cucumber and tomatoes, and divide the chicken strips among them. Spoon over a little yogurt chutney and serve.

Spiced Chicken Koftas

Koftas are spicy balls of minced poultry or meat. In this recipe
they are made with chicken, but you could use lamb or beef. Lime pickle
is available in Asian food stores and some supermarkets.

4 Drain on paper towels and serve
with lime pickle and lime wedges.

Serves 4
500 g/1 lb skinless, boneless chicken, chopped coarsely
1 garlic clove
2.5 cm/1 inch piece fresh ginger root, grated
1/2 green pepper, deseeded and chopped coarsely
2 fresh green chillies, deseeded and chopped
4 tsp garam masala
1/2 tsp ground turmeric
2 tbsp chopped fresh coriander
1/2 tsp salt
6 tbsp vegetable oil
lime pickle and lime wedges, to serve

1 Put all the ingredients except the
oil and lime pickle into a food
processor or blender and process until
the mixture is chopped finely.
Alternatively, chop the chicken, garlic,
ginger, pepper and chillies very finely,
and mix together in a bowl with the
garam masala, turmeric, coriander
and salt.

2 Shape the mixture between the
palms of your hands to form 16 small
evenly-shaped balls.

3 Heat the oil in a wok or large frying
pan and fry the koftas for 8–10
minutes, turning occasionally. If you
cannot fit all the koftas into the pan
at once, keep the first batch warm in a
low oven, while you fry the remaining
koftas.

Thai Chicken Spring Rolls

A cucumber dipping sauce tastes perfect with these delicious spring rolls,
filled with chicken and fresh, crunchy vegetables.

Serves 4
1 tbsp light soy sauce
1 tsp sugar
2 tsp cornflour, blended with 2 tbsp cold water
2 tbsp vegetable oil
4 spring onions, trimmed and sliced very finely
1 carrot, cut into matchstick pieces
1 small green or red pepper, sliced finely
60 g/2 oz button mushrooms, sliced
60 g/2 oz bean-sprouts
175 g/6 oz cooked skinless, boneless chicken, shredded
12 × 20 cm/8 inch spring roll wrappers
oil for deep-frying
salt and pepper
spring onion brushes, to garnish

DIPPING SAUCE

50 ml/2 fl oz light malt vinegar
2 tbsp water
60 g/2 oz light muscovado sugar
$^1/_2$ tsp salt
5 cm/2 inch piece of cucumber, peeled and chopped finely
4 spring onions, trimmed and sliced finely
1 small red or green chilli, deseeded and chopped very finely

1 Mix together the soy sauce, sugar and cornflour paste.

2 Heat the oil in a wok or frying pan and add the spring onions, carrot and pepper. Stir-fry for 2–3 minutes. Add the mushrooms, bean-sprouts and chicken and cook for a further 2 minutes. Season with salt and pepper.

3 Add the cornflour mixture to the stir-fry and cook, stirring continuously for about 1 minute, until thickened. Leave to cool.

4 Place spoonfuls of the chicken mixture on to the spring roll wrappers. Dampen the edges and roll them up to enclose the filling.

5 To make the dipping sauce, heat the vinegar, water, sugar and salt in a saucepan. Boil for 1 minute. Mix the cucumber, spring onions and chilli in a small serving bowl and pour over the vinegar mixture. Cool.

6 Heat the oil and fry the rolls until crisp and golden brown. Drain on paper towels, then serve, garnished with spring onion brushes and accompanied by the cucumber dipping sauce.

Chicken Scallops

Served in scallop shells, this dish makes a stylish
presentation for a dinner-party first course.

Serves 4
175 g/6 oz short-cut macaroni, or other short dried pasta shapes
3 tbsp vegetable oil, plus extra for brushing
1 onion, chopped finely
3 slices unsmoked collar or back bacon, derinded and chopped
125 g/4 oz button mushrooms, sliced thinly
175 g/6 oz cooked skinless, boneless chicken, diced
175 ml/6 fl oz crème fraîche
4 tbsp dry breadcrumbs
60 g/2 oz mature Cheddar, grated
salt and pepper
sprigs of flat-leaf parsley, to garnish

1 Cook the pasta in a large pan of boiling salted water to which you have added 1 tablespoon of the oil. When the pasta is almost tender, drain through a colander, return to the pan and cover.

2 Heat the remaining oil in a pan over medium heat and fry the onion until it is translucent. Add the chopped bacon and mushrooms and cook for a further 3–4 minutes, stirring once or twice.

3 Stir in the drained pasta, diced chicken and the crème fraîche, and season to taste.

4 Brush four large scallop shells with oil. Spoon in the chicken mixture and smooth to make neat mounds.

5 Mix together the breadcrumbs and cheese, and sprinkle over the top of the shells. Press the topping lightly into the chicken mixture, and place under a preheated medium grill for 4–5 minutes, until golden brown and bubbling. Garnish with parsley sprigs, and serve hot.

Chicken Pepperonata

All the sunshine colours and flavours of the Mediterranean
are combined in this easy dish.

Serves 4
8 skinless chicken thighs
2 tbsp wholemeal flour
2 tbsp olive oil
1 small onion, sliced thinly
1 garlic clove, crushed
1 each large red, yellow and green peppers, sliced thinly
425 g/14 oz can chopped tomatoes
1 tbsp chopped oregano
salt and pepper
fresh oregano, to garnish

1 Remove the skin from the chicken thighs and toss in the flour.

2 Heat the oil in a wide pan and fry the chicken quickly until sealed and lightly browned, then remove from the pan. Add the onion to the pan and gently fry until soft. Add the garlic, peppers, tomatoes and oregano, then bring to the boil, stirring.

3 Arrange the chicken over the vegetables, season well with salt and pepper, then cover the pan tightly and simmer for 20–25 minutes or until the chicken is completely cooked through and tender.

4 Season to taste, garnish with oregano and serve with crusty wholemeal bread.

COOK'S TIP

For extra flavour, halve the peppers and grill under a preheated grill until the skins are charred. Leave to cool then remove the skins and seeds. Slice the peppers thinly and use in the recipe.

Chicken Pan Bagna

Perfect for a picnic or packed lunch, this Mediterranean-style
sandwich can be prepared ahead.

Serves 6
1 long French stick
1 garlic clove
120 ml/4 floz olive oil
20 g/$^3/_4$ oz can anchovy fillets
350 g/12 oz cold roast chicken
2 large tomatoes, sliced
8 large, pitted black olives, chopped
pepper

1 Cut the French stick in half
lengthways and open out.

2 Cut the garlic clove in half and rub
over the bread. Sprinkle the cut
surface of the bread with the oil.

3 Drain the anchovies, thinly slice
the chicken and arrange over the
bread with the tomatoes.

4 Scatter with black olives and plenty
of pepper. Sandwich the loaf back
together and wrap tightly in foil until
required. Cut into slices to serve.

COOK'S TIP

Arrange a few fresh basil leaves in
between the tomato slices to add a
warm, spicy flavour. Use a good quality
olive oil in this recipe for extra flavour.

Oaty Chicken Pieces

A very low-fat chicken recipe with a refreshingly light, mustard-spiced sauce, which is ideal for a healthy lunchbox or a light meal with salad.

Serves 4
30 g/1 oz rolled oats
1 tbsp chopped fresh rosemary
4 skinless chicken quarters
1 egg white
150 g/5 oz natural low-fat fromage frais
2 tsp wholegrain mustard
salt and pepper

1 Mix together the oats, rosemary and salt and pepper.

2 Brush each piece of chicken evenly with egg white, then coat in the oat mixture. Place on a baking sheet and bake in a preheated oven, 200°C/400°F/Gas Mark 6, for about 40 minutes or until the juices run clear when the chicken is pierced.

3 Mix together the fromage frais and mustard, season to taste then serve with the chicken, hot or cold, with a grated carrot salad.

COOK'S VARIATION

Instead of chicken quarters, use skinless, boneless chicken breasts, which are easier to slice. Reduce the cooking time by about 10 minutes and test for doneness.

Chicken & Cheese Jackets

Use the breasts from a roasted chicken for this delicious, healthy snack.

Serves 4
4 large baking potatoes
250 g/8 oz cooked, boneless chicken breasts
4 spring onions
250 g/8 oz low-fat soft cheese or Quark
pepper

1 Scrub the potatoes and prick them all over with a fork. Bake in a preheated oven, 200°C/400°F/Gas Mark 6, for about 50 minutes until tender, or cook in a microwave on High/100% power for 12–15 minutes.

2 Dice the chicken, trim and thickly slice the spring onions and mix with the low-fat soft cheese.

3 Cut a cross through the top of each potato and pull slightly apart. Spoon the chicken filling into the potatoes and sprinkle with pepper. Serve immediately with coleslaw, green salad or a mixed salad.

COOK'S TIP

Look for Quark in the chilled section. It is a low-fat, white, fresh curd cheese made from cow's milk with a delicate, slightly sour flavour.

Cheesy Garlic Drummers

Ideal for informal parties, these tasty chicken drumsticks can be prepared
for cooking a day in advance. Instead of baking the chicken drumsticks,
you could cook them on the barbecue instead.

Serves 6

15 g/¹/₂ oz/1 tbsp butter

1 garlic clove, crushed

3 tbsp chopped fresh parsley

125 g/4 oz
ricotta cheese

4 tbsp grated Parmesan cheese

3 tbsp fresh breadcrumbs

12 chicken drumsticks

salt and pepper

lemon slices, to garnish

1 Melt the butter and fry the garlic gently without browning, stirring for 1 minute.

2 Remove from the heat and stir in the parsley, the cheeses, breadcrumbs and seasoning.

3 Carefully loosen the skin around the chicken drumsticks.

4 Push about a tablespoon of the stuffing under the skin of each drumstick. Arrange the drumsticks in a wide baking tin.

5 Bake in a preheated oven, 190°C/375°F/ Gas Mark 5, for about 45 minutes until golden. Serve hot or cold, garnished with lemon slices.

COOK'S TIP

Any strongly flavoured cheese can be used instead of the Parmesan. Try a matured Cheddar cheese or use another Italian cheese; pecorino.

Old English Spicy Chicken Salad

For this simple, refreshing summer salad you can use leftover roast chicken, or ready-roasted chicken to save time. Add the dressing just before serving, or the spinach will lose its crispness if left in the dressing for too long.

Serves 4

250 g/8 oz young spinach leaves

3 sticks celery,
sliced thinly

1/2 cucumber, sliced thinly

2 spring onions,
sliced thinly

3 tbsp chopped fresh parsley

350g/12oz boneless,
roast chicken, sliced thinly

DRESSING

2.5 cm/1inch piece fresh ginger
root, grated finely

3 tbsp olive oil

1 tbsp white wine vinegar

1 tbsp clear honey

1/2 tsp ground cinnamon

salt and pepper

smoked almonds,
to garnish (optional)

1 Thoroughly wash and dry the spinach leaves.

2 Toss the celery, cucumber and spring onions with the spinach and parsley in a large bowl.

3 Transfer to serving plates and arrange the chicken over the salad.

4 In a screw-topped jar, combine all the dressing ingredients and shake well to mix.

5 Season to taste then pour over the salad. Scatter a few smoked almonds over the salad to garnish, if using.

Sticky Chicken Drummers with Mango Salsa

Delicious served hot or cold, and any leftover chicken can be packed in lunchboxes for a tasty alternative to sandwiches.

Serves 4
8 skinless chicken drumsticks
3 tbsp mango chutney
2 tsp Dijon mustard
2 tsp oil
1 tsp paprika
1 tsp black mustard seeds, roughly crushed
$1/2$ tsp turmeric
2 garlic cloves, chopped
salt and pepper

SALSA

1 mango, diced
1 tomato, chopped finely
$1/2$ red onion, sliced thinly
2 tbsp chopped fresh coriander

1 Using a small, sharp knife, slash each drumstick three or four times then place in a roasting tin.

2 Mix together the mango chutney, mustard, oil, spices, garlic and salt and pepper and spoon over the chicken drumsticks, turning until they are coated all over with the glaze.

3 Cook in a preheated oven, 200°C/400°F/Gas Mark 6, for 40 minutes, brushing with the glaze several times during cooking until the chicken is well browned and the juices run clear when pierced with a skewer.

4 Meanwhile, mix together the mango, tomato, onion and coriander for the mango salsa. Season to taste and chill until needed.

5 Arrange the chicken drumsticks on a serving plate and serve hot or cold with the mango salsa.

COOK'S VARIATION

Use mild curry powder instead of the turmeric.

Solomongundy

This recipe is ideally suited as a cold platter for a buffet party or a spectacular starter for a special meal.

Serves 4
1 large lettuce
4 chicken breasts, cooked and sliced thinly
8 rollmop herrings and their marinade
6 hard-boiled eggs, quartered
125 g/4 oz cooked ham, sliced
125 g/4 oz roast beef, sliced
125 g/4 oz roast lamb, sliced
150 g/6 oz mangetout, cooked
125 g/4 oz seedless black grapes,
20 stuffed olives, sliced
12 shallots, boiled
60 g/2 oz/$^{1}/_{2}$ cup flaked almonds
60 g/2 oz/$^{1}/_{3}$ cup sultanas
2 oranges
sprig of mint
salt and pepper

1 Spread out the lettuce leaves on a large oval platter.

2 Arrange the chicken in three sections or lines on the platter.

3 Place the roll mops, eggs and meats in lines or sections over the remainder of the platter.

4 Use the mangetout, grapes, olives, shallots, almonds and sultanas to fill in the spaces between the sections.

5 Grate the rind from the oranges and sprinkle over the whole platter. Peel and slice the oranges and add the orange slices, mint sprig to the platter. Season well.

6 Finally, sprinkle with the marinade from the herrings and serve with fresh crusty bread.

COOK'S VARIATION

Should you wish, serve with cold, cooked vegetables, such as sliced beans, baby sweetcorn and cooked beetroot.

Potted Smoked Chicken

This recipe can be made a few days ahead and kept chilled until needed.
A food processor makes light work of blending the ingredients,
but you can pound by hand for a more coarse mixture.

Serves 4–6
350g/12 oz
chopped smoked chicken
pinch each of grated nutmeg and mace
125 g/4 oz butter, softened
2 tbsp port
2 tbsp double cream
salt and pepper

1 Place the smoked chicken in a large bowl with all the ingredients, and season well.

2 Pound until the mixture is very smooth or blend in a food processor.

3 Transfer the mixture to individual earthenware pots or one large pot.

4 Cover with buttered greaseproof paper and weight down with cans or weights.

5 Chill for 4 hours.

6 Remove the paper and cover with clarified butter (see Cook's Tip).

7 Serve with slices of brown bread and fresh butter.

COOK'S TIP

To make clarified butter:
Place 250 g/8 oz butter in a saucepan and heat gently, skimming off the foam as the butter heats.
The sediment sinks to the bottom of the pan as the butter heats. When completely melted, remove the pan from the heat and leave it to stand for a least 4 minutes. Strain the butter through a piece of muslin into a bowl. Allow the butter to cool a little before pouring it over the surface of the potted chicken.

Chicken & Herb Fritters

These fritters are delicious served with a green salad,
a fresh vegetable salsa or a chilli sauce dip.

Makes 8
500 g/1lb mashed potato, with butter added
250 g/8 oz chopped, cooked chicken
125 g/4 oz cooked ham, chopped finely
1 tbsp mixed herbs
2 eggs, lightly beaten
milk
125 g/4 oz fresh brown breadcrumbs
oil for shallow frying
salt and pepper

1 In a large bowl, blend the potatoes, chicken, ham, herbs and 1 egg, and season well.

2 Shape the mixture into small balls or flat pancakes.

3 Add a little milk to the second egg.

4 Place the breadcrumbs on a plate. Dip the balls in the egg and milk mixture then roll in the breadcrumbs, to coat them completely.

5 Heat the cooking oil in a large frying pan and cook the fritters until they are golden brown.

COOK'S TIP

A mixture of chopped fresh tarragon and parsley make a fresh and flavourful addition to these fritters.

Chicken Rarebit

A tasty snack that can be served alone as a snack or to accompany a light, clear soup.

Serves 4
250 g/8 oz grated Wensleydale
250 g/8 oz shredded, cooked chicken
1 tbsp butter
1 tbsp Worcestershire sauce
1 tsp dry English mustard
2 tsp plain flour
4 tbsp mild beer
4 slices of bread, toasted on both sides
salt and pepper
1 tbsp chopped fresh parsley, to garnish

1 Place the cheese, chicken, butter, Worcestershire sauce, mustard, flour and beer in a small saucepan. Mix together and season.

2 Gently bring the mixture to the boil and remove from the heat immediately.

3 Beat until the mixture becomes creamy in texture, and allow to cool.

4 Toast the bread and spread with the chicken mixture. Place under a hot grill until bubbling and golden brown.

5 Sprinkle with a little parsley and serve with cherry tomatoes.

Coronation Chicken

This classic salad is good as a starter or as part of a buffet.
Mango chutney makes a tasty addition.

Serves 6
4 tbsp olive oil
900 g/2lb chicken meat, diced
125 g/4 oz rindless, smoked bacon, diced
12 shallots
2 garlic cloves, crushed
1 tbsp mild curry powder
300 ml/$\frac{1}{2}$ pint mayonniase
1 tbsp runny honey
1 tbsp chopped fresh parsley
90 g/3 oz seedless black grapes, quartered
pepper

1 Heat the oil in a large frying pan add the chicken, bacon, shallots, garlic and curry powder. Cook slowly for about 15 minutes.

2 With a slotted spoon, spoon the mixture into a clean mixing bowl

3 Allow the mixture to cool completely then season well.

4 Blend the mayonnaise with a little honey, then add the parsley.

5 Toss the chicken in the mixture.

6 Place the mixture in a deep serving dish, garnish with the grapes and serve with cold saffron rice.

Chicken with Pear & Blue Cheese Salad

The combination of chicken, blue cheese and pears is delicious in this warm salad.

Serves 6
50 ml/2 fl oz olive oil
6 shallots, sliced
1 garlic clove, crushed
2 tbsp chopped fresh tarragon
1 tbsp English mustard
6 skinless, boneless chicken breasts
1 tbsp flour
150 ml/$^1/_4$ pint chicken stock
1 apple, diced finely
1 tbsp chopped walnuts
2 tbsp double cream
salt and pepper

SALAD
250 g/8 oz cooked rice
2 large pears, diced
150 g/5 oz blue cheese, diced
1 red pepper, diced
1 tbsp chopped fresh coriander
1 tbsp sesame oil

1 Place the olive oil, shallots, garlic, tarragon and mustard in a deep bowl. Season well and mix the ingredients together thoroughly.

2 Place the chicken in the marinade, cover with cling film and chill in the refrigerator for about 4 hours.

3 Drain the chicken, reserving the marinade. Quickly fry the chicken in a large, deep non-stick frying pan for 4 minutes on both sides. Remove the chicken from the pan to a warm serving dish. Meanwhile add the marinade to the pan, bring to the boil and sprinkle with the flour. Add the

chicken stock, apple and walnuts and gently simmer for 5 minutes. Return the chicken to the sauce, add the cream and cook for 2 minutes.

4 Mix the salad ingredients together, place a little on each plate and top with a chicken breast and a spoonful of the sauce.

Waldorf Summer Chicken Salad

This colourful and healthy dish is a variation of a classic salad.

Serves 4
500 g/1lb red apples, diced
3 tbsp fresh lemon juice
150 ml/¼ pint light mayonnaise
1 head of celery
4 shallots, sliced
1 garlic clove, crushed
90 g/3 oz walnuts, chopped
500 g/1 lb cooked chicken, cubed
1 Cos lettuce
pepper
sliced apple and walnuts, to garnish

1 Place the apples in a bowl with the lemon juice and 1 tablespoon of mayonnaise. Leave for 40 minutes.

2 Slice the celery very thinly.

3 Add the celery with the shallots, garlic and walnuts to the apple, mix and then add the remaining mayonnaise and blend thoroughly.

4 Add the chicken, mix, and line a glass salad bowl or serving dish with the lettuce. Pile the chicken salad into the centre, sprinkle with pepper and garnish with apple slices and walnuts.

COOK'S TIP

Instead of the shallots, use spring onions for a milder flavour. Trim the spring onions and slice finely.

Spiced Chicken & Grape Salad

Tender chicken breast, sweet grapes and crisp celery coated in a mild curry
mayonnaise make a wonderful al fresco lunch.

Serves 4

500 g/1 lb cooked skinless,
boneless chicken breasts

2 celery sticks, sliced finely

250 g/8 oz black grapes

60 g/2 oz split almonds,
toasted

pinch of paprika

sprigs of fresh coriander
or flat-leafed parsley, to garnish

CURRY SAUCE

150 ml/¼ pint
mayonnaise

125 g/4 oz natural
fromage frais

1 tbsp clear honey

1 tbsp curry paste

1 Cut the chicken into fairly large pieces and transfer to a bowl with the sliced celery.

2 Halve the grapes, remove the seeds and add to the bowl.

3 To make the curry sauce, mix the mayonnaise, fromage frais, honey and curry paste together until blended.

4 Pour the curry sauce over the salad and mix together carefully until well coated.

5 Transfer to a shallow serving dish and sprinkle with the almonds and paprika. Garnish with the coriander (cilantro) or parsley.

Roasts & Bakes

The aroma of roasting chicken is always tempting and in this section there are a wealth of delightful recipes. Traditional roast chicken is included, with all the trimmings, as well as many other imaginative treatments. Unusual stuffings add interest – try courgette and lime, or oat and herb stuffing. Many of the recipes in this section exploit the complementary

flavours of chicken and fruits and there are some enticing taste combinations including cranberries, mango, black cherries, dried apples, peaches, plums, oranges and mangoes. There are chicken pieces wrapped in bacon, stuffed with ham and cheese, or brushed with honey and mustard. Whole chickens are sprinkled with seeds or cooked with fresh young vegetables. Tasty stuffings are tucked just under the skin to impart flavour and there are boned, easy-to-slice chicken dishes.

Roast Chicken with Coriander & Garlic

This recipe for chicken is coated with a fresh-flavoured marinade then roasted.
Try serving it with rice, yogurt and salad.

Serves 4–6
3 sprigs fresh coriander, chopped
4 garlic cloves
1/2 tsp salt
1 tsp pepper
4 tbsp lemon juice
4 tbsp olive oil
1 large chicken
pepper

1 Place the chopped coriander, garlic, salt, pepper, lemon juice and olive oil in a pestle and mortar and pound together or blend in a food processor.

2 Chill the mixture for 4 hours to allow the flavour to mature.

3 Place the chicken in a roasting tin. Coat generously with the coriander and garlic mixture.

4 Sprinkle with pepper and roast in a preheated oven, 190°C/375°F/Gas Mark 5, on a low shelf for about 1½ hours, basting every 20 minutes with the coriander mixture. If the chicken starts to look brown, cover with foil.

COOK'S VARIATION

Any fresh herb can be used in this recipe instead of the coriander. Tarragon or thyme are a good combination with chicken.

Breast of Chicken with York Ham & Stilton Cheese

Beetroot is one of the most underrated vegetables, adding flavour and colour to numerous dishes. Tender young beetroot are used in this recipe.

Serves 4
4 chicken supremes
8 fresh sage leaves
8 thin slices of York ham
250g/8 oz Stilton cheese, cut into 8 slices
8 slices rindless streaky bacon
150 ml/1¼ pint chicken stock
2 tbsp port
24 shallots
500 g/1 lb baby beetroot, cooked
1 tbsp cornflour, blended with a little port
salt and pepper

1 Cut a long slit horizontally along each chicken breast to make a pocket.

2 Insert 2 sage leaves into each pocket and season lightly.

3 Wrap each slice of ham around a slice of cheese and place 2 into each chicken pocket.

4 Carefully wrap enough bacon around each breast to completely cover the pockets containing the cheese and ham.

5 Place the breasts in an ovenproof casserole dish and pour over the chicken stock and port.

6 Add the shallots, cover with a lid or cooking foil and braise in a preheated oven, 190°C/375°F/Gas Mark 5, for about 40 minutes.

7 Carefully place each breast onto a cutting board and slice through them to create a fan effect. Serve them on a warm serving dish with the shallots and beetroot.

8 Put the juices from the casserole into a saucepan and bring to the boil, remove from the heat and add the cornflour paste. Gently simmer and cook the sauce for 2 minutes, then pour over the shallots and beetroot.

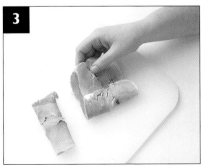

Pot Roast Orange & Sesame

This colourful, nutritious pot-roast could be served for a family meal or for a special dinner.
Add more vegetables if you're feeding a crowd – if your roasting pot is large enough!

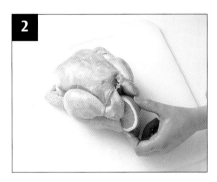

Serves 4
2 tbsp sunflower oil
1 chicken, weighing about 1.5 kg/3 lb
2 large oranges
2 small onions, quartered
500 g/1 lb small whole carrots or thin carrots, cut into 5 cm/2 inch lengths
150ml/¼ pint orange juice
2 tbsp brandy
2 tbsp sesame seeds
1 tbsp cornflour
salt and pepper

1 Heat the oil in a large flameproof casserole and fry the chicken, turning occasionally until evenly browned.

2 Cut one orange in half and place half inside the cavity of the chicken. Place the chicken in a large, deep casserole. Arrange the onions and carrots around the chicken.

3 Season with salt and pepper and pour over the orange juice.

4 Cut the remaining oranges into thin wedges and tuck around the chicken, among the vegetables.

5 Cover and cook in a preheated oven, 180°C/350°F/Gas Mark 4, for about 1½ hours, or until there is no trace of pink in the chicken juices when pierced, and the vegetables are tender. Remove the lid and sprinkle with the brandy and sesame seeds,

and return to the oven for 10 minutes.

6 To serve, lift the chicken onto a large platter and add the vegetables. Skim any excess fat from the juices. Blend the cornflour with 1 tablespoon

cold water, then stir into the juices and bring to the boil, stirring all the time. Adjust to taste, then serve the sauce with the chicken.

Poussin with Dried Fruits

Baby chickens are ideal for a one or two portion meal, and cook very easily and quickly for a special dinner. If you're cooking for one and it's not worth putting the oven on, a microwave makes cooking even quicker and more convenient. Use any mixture of dried fruits for a rich fruity flavour and colourful effect.

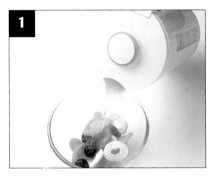

Serves 2
125 g/4 oz dried apples, peaches and prunes
120 ml/4 floz boiling water
2 baby chickens
30 g/1 oz walnut halves
1 tbsp honey
1 tsp ground allspice
1 tbsp walnut oil
salt and pepper

6 Serve hot with fresh vegetables and new potatoes.

COOK'S TIP

Alternative dried fruits that can be used in this recipe are cherries, mangoes or pawpaws.

1 Place the fruits in a bowl, cover with the water and leave to stand for about 30 minutes.

2 Cut the chickens in half down the breastbone using a sharp knife, or leave whole.

3 Mix the fruit and any juices with the walnuts, honey and allspice and divide between two small roasting bags or squares of foil.

4 Brush the chickens with walnut oil and sprinkle with salt and pepper then place on top of the fruits.

5 Close the roasting bags or fold the foil over to enclose the chickens and bake on a baking sheet in a preheated oven, 190°C/375°F/Gas Mark 5, for 25–30 minutes or until the juices run clear. To cook in a microwave, use microwave roasting bags and cook on high/100% power for 6–7 minutes each, depending on size.

Supreme of Chicken with Black Cherries

This recipe is rather time-consuming but it is well worth the effort.
Cherries and chicken make a good flavour combination.

Serves 6
6 large chicken supremes
6 black peppercorns, crushed
300 g/10 oz pitted black cherries, or canned pitted cherries
12 shallots, sliced
4 slices rindless. streaky bacon, chopped
8 juniper berries
4 tbsp port
150 ml/¼ pint red wine
30 g/1 oz/2 tbsp butter
2 tbsp walnut oil
30 g/1 oz flour
salt and pepper
black cherries and parsley, to garnish

1 Place the chicken in a large deep baking tin. Add the peppercorns, cherries or canned cherries, and their juice, if using, and the shallots.

2 Add the bacon, juniper berries, port and wine. Season well.

3 Place the chicken and marinade in the fridge for 48 hours.

4 Heat the butter and walnut oil in a large frying pan. Remove the chicken from the marinade and fry quickly in the pan for 4 minutes on each side.

5 Return the chicken to the marinade, reserving the butter, oil and juices in the pan.

6 Cover with foil and bake in a preheated oven, 180°C/350°F/Gas Mark 4, for 20 minutes. Transfer the chicken from the baking tin to a warm serving dish. Add the flour to the juices in the frying pan and cook for 4 minutes, add the marinade and bring to the boil then simmer for 10 minutes until the sauce is smooth.

7 Pour the sauce over the chicken supremes and garnish with black cherries and fresh parsley.

Roast Chicken in Wild Mushroom Sauce

This unusual chicken dish has the flavour of roast chicken but is finished off in a casserole with a wild mushroom sauce.

Serves 4
90 g/3 oz butter, softened
1 garlic clove, crushed
1 large chicken
175 g/6 oz wild mushrooms
12 shallots
30 g/1 oz plain flour
150 ml/¹/₄ pint brandy
300 ml/¹/₄ pint double cream
salt and pepper
1 tbsp chopped fresh parsley, to garnish

1 Place the butter, garlic, and salt and pepper in a bowl.

2 Rub the mixture inside and outside of the chicken and leave for 2 hours.

3 Place the chicken in a large roasting tin and roast in the centre of a preheated oven, 230°C/450°F/Gas Mark 8, for 1¹/₂ hours, basting every ten minutes.

4 Remove the chicken from the roasting tin and set aside to cool slightly.

5 Transfer the chicken juices to a saucepan and cook the mushrooms and shallots for 5 minutes. Sprinkle with the flour. Add the warm brandy and ignite.

6 Add the cream and cook for 3 minutes on a very low heat, stirring all the time.

7 Remove the bones and cut the chicken into small bite-sized pieces, then place the meat in a casserole dish. Cover with the mushroom sauce and bake in the oven, with the heat reduced to 160°C/325°F/Gas Mark 3, for a further 12 minutes. Garnish with the parsley and serve with wild rice or roast potatoes, and Brussel sprouts.

Honey & Mustard Baked Chicken

Chicken portions are brushed with a classic combination of honey and
mustard then a crunchy coating of poppy seeds is added.

Serves 4
8 chicken portions
60 g/2 oz butter, melted
4 tbsp mild mustard
4 tbsp clear honey
2 tbsp lemon juice
1 tsp paprika
3 tbsp poppy seeds
salt and pepper

1 Place the chicken pieces, skinless side down, on a large baking tray.

2 Place all the ingredients except the poppy seeds into a large bowl and blend together thoroughly.

3 Using a pastry brush, paint the mixture over the chicken portions.

4 Bake in the centre of a preheated oven, 200°C/400°F/Gas Mark 6, for 15 minutes.

5 Carefully turn over the chicken pieces, coating the top side of the chicken again.

6 Sprinkle the chicken with poppy seeds and return to the oven for a further 15 minutes.

7 Arrange the chicken on a serving dish, pour over the cooking juices and serve with a crisp salad.

Californian Chicken

It is better if you have time to bone the chicken completely,
or use chicken breast after removing all the fat and skin.

Serves 4–6
175 g/6 oz plain flour
1 tsp paprika
1 tsp freeze-dried Italian seasoning
1 tsp freeze-dried tarragon
1 tsp rosemary, finely crushed
2 eggs, beaten
120 ml/4 fl oz milk
1 chicken, weighing about 2 kg/4 lb, jointed
seasoned flour
150 ml/¼ pint rapeseed oil
2 bananas, quartered
1 apple, cut into rings,
350 g/12 oz can sweetcorn & peppers, drained
oil for frying
salt and pepper

1 Mix together the flour, salt, spices and herbs in a large bowl. Make a well in the centre and add the eggs.

2 Blend and slowly add the milk, whisking until very smooth.

3 Coat the chicken pieces with seasoned flour and dip the chicken pieces into the batter mix.

4 Heat the oil in a large frying pan. Add the chicken and fry for about 3 minutes or until lightly browned all over. Place the chicken pieces on a non-stick baking tray.

5 Batter the bananas and apple rings and fry for 2 minutes.

6 Finally, toss the sweetcorn into the leftover batter.

7 Heat a little oil in a frying pan. Drop in spoonfuls of the sweetcorn mixture to make flat patty cakes. Cook for 4 minutes on each side. Keep warm with the apple and banana fritters.

8 Bake the chicken in a preheated oven, 200°C/400°F/Gas Mark 6, for

25 minutes until the chicken is tender and golden brown.

9 Arrange the chicken, sweetcorn fritters, and the apple and banana fritters on a bed of fresh watercress. Serve with a peppercorn or horseradish sauce.

Springtime Roast Chicken

Baby chickens are simple to prepare, take about 30 minutes to roast and can be easily cut in half lengthways with a sharp knife. One baby chicken makes a substantial serving for each person. This combination of baby vegetables and baby chickens with a tangy low-fat sauce makes a healthy meal.

Serves 4
5 tbsp fresh brown breadcrumbs
200 g/7 oz fromage frais or low-fat crème fraîche
5 tbsp chopped fresh parsley
5 tbsp chopped fresh chives
4 baby chickens
1 tbsp sunflower oil
675 g/1½ lb young spring vegetables such as carrots, courgettes, sugar snap peas, corn and turnips, cut into small chunks
120 ml/4 floz boiling chicken stock
2 tsp cornflour
150 ml/¼ pint dry white wine
salt and pepper

1 Mix together the breadcrumbs, one-third of the fromage frais and 2 tablespoons each of parsley and chives. Season well then spoon into the neck ends of the baby chickens. Place the chickens on a rack in a roasting tin, brush with oil and season well.

2 Roast in a preheated oven, 220°C/425°F/Gas Mark 7, for 30–35 minutes or until the juices run clear, not pink, when the chickens are pierced with a skewer.

3 Place the vegetables in a shallow ovenproof dish in one layer and add half the remaining herbs with the stock. Cover and bake for 25–30 minutes until tender. Lift the chickens onto a serving plate and skim any fat from the juices in the tin. Add the vegetable juices.

4 Blend the cornflour with the wine and whisk into the sauce with the remaining fromage frais. Whisk until boiling, then add the remaining herbs. Season to taste. Spoon the sauce over the chickens and serve with the vegetables.

Mediterranean Style Sunday Roast

A roast that is full of Mediterranean flavour. A mixture of feta cheese, rosemary
and sun-dried tomatoes is stuffed under the chicken skin,
then roasted with garlic, new potatoes and vegetables.

Serves 6
2.5 kg/5¹/₂ lb chicken
sprigs of fresh rosemary
175 g/6 oz feta cheese, coarsely grated
2 tbsp sun-dried tomato paste
60 g/2 oz butter, softened
1 bulb garlic
1 kg/2 lb new potatoes, halved if large
1 each red, green and yellow pepper, cut into chunks
3 courgettes, sliced thinly
2 tbsp olive oil
2 tbsp plain flour
600 ml/1pint chicken stock
salt and pepper

1 Rinse the chicken inside and out with cold water and drain well. Carefully cut between the skin and the top of the breast meat using a small pointed knife. Slide a finger into the slit and carefully enlarge it to form a pocket. Continue until the skin is completely lifted away from both breasts and the top of the legs.

2 Chop the leaves from 3 rosemary stems. Mix with the feta, sun-dried tomato paste, butter and pepper then spoon under the skin. Put the chicken in a large roasting tin, cover with foil and cook in a preheated oven, 190°C/375°F/Gas Mark 5, for 20 minutes per 500g/1lb plus 20 minutes.

3 Break the garlic bulb into cloves but do not peel. Add the vegetables to the chicken after 40 minutes.

4 Drizzle with oil, tuck in a few stems of rosemary and season well. Cook for the remaining time, removing the foil for the last 40 minutes to brown the chicken.

5 Transfer the chicken to a serving platter. Place some of the vegetables around the chicken and transfer the remainder to a warmed serving dish. Pour the fat out of the roasting tin and stir the flour into the remaining pan juices. Cook for 2 minutes then gradually stir in the stock. Bring to the boil, stirring until thickened and smooth. Strain into a sauce boat and garnish the chicken with rosemary.

Pollo Catalan

The Catalan region of Spain is famous for its wonderful combinations of meat with fruit. Nuts and spices are often added too. In this recipe, peaches lend a touch of sweetness and pine nuts, cinnamon and sherry add an unusual twist. Canned peach halves in natural juice make an easy storecupboard alternative.

Serves 6
60 g/2 oz fresh brown breadcrumbs
60 g/2 oz pine nuts
1 small egg, beaten
4 tbsp chopped fresh thyme or 1 tbsp dried thyme
4 fresh peaches or 8 canned peach halves
1 chicken, weighing about 2 5 kg/5½ lb
1 tsp ground cinnamon
200 ml/7 fl oz Amontillado sherry
4 tbsp double cream
salt and pepper

1 Combine the breadcrumbs with 30 g/1 oz pine nuts, the egg and the thyme.

2 Halve and stone the fresh peaches, and remove the skin if necessary. Dice one peach into small pieces and stir into the breadcrumb mixture. Season well with salt and pepper. Spoon the stuffing into the neck cavity of the chicken, securing the skin firmly over it.

3 Place the chicken in a roasting tin and sprinkle the cinnamon over the skin.

4 Cover loosely with foil and roast in a preheated oven, 190°C/375°F/Gas Mark 5, for 1 hour, basting occasionally.

5 Remove the foil and spoon the sherry over the chicken. Cook for a further 30 minutes, basting with the sherry juices, until the juices run clear when the chicken is pierced with a skewer. Sprinkle the remaining pine nuts over the remaining peach halves and place in an ovenproof dish in the oven for the final 10 minutes of cooking time.

6 Lift the chicken onto a serving plate and arrange the peaches around it. Skim any fat from the juices, stir in the cream and heat gently. Serve with the chicken.

Whisky Roast Chicken

An unusual change from a plain roast, with a distinctly warming Scottish
flavour and a delicious oatmeal stuffing.

Serves 6
1 chicken, weighing 2 kg/4 lb
1 tbsp heather honey
2 tbsp Scotch whisky
2 tbsp plain flour
300 ml/½ pint
chicken stock

STUFFING
1 medium onion, finely chopped
1 stick celery, sliced thinly
1 tbsp butter or sunflower oil
1 tsp dried thyme
4 tbsp porridge oats
4 tbsp chicken stock
salt and pepper

1 To make the stuffing, fry the onion and celery in the butter or oil, stirring over a moderate heat until softened and lightly browned.

2 Remove from the heat and stir in the thyme, oats, stock, salt and pepper.

3 Stuff the neck end of the chicken with the mixture and tuck the neck flap under. Place in a roasting tin, brush lightly with oil, and roast in a preheated oven, 190°C/375°F/Gas Mark 5, for about 1 hour.

4 Mix the honey with 1 tablespoon whisky and brush the mixture over the chicken. Return to the oven for a further 20 minutes, or until the chicken is golden brown and the juices run clear when pierced through the thickest part with a skewer.

5 Lift the chicken onto a serving plate. Skim the fat from the juices then stir in the flour. Stir over a moderate heat until the mixture bubbles, then gradually add the stock and remaining whisky.

6 Bring to the boil, stirring, then simmer for 1 minute and serve the chicken with the sauce, green vegetable and sauté potatoes.

Gardener's Chicken

Any combination of small, young vegetables can be roasted with the chicken,
such as courgettes, leeks and onions.

Serves 4
250 g/8 oz parsnips, peeled and chopped
125 g/4 oz carrots, peeled and chopped
30 g/1 oz fresh breadcrumbs
$^1/_4$ tsp grated nutmeg
1 tbsp chopped fresh parsley
1.5 kg/3 lb chicken
bunch parsley
$^1/_2$ onion
30 g/1 oz butter, softened
4 tbsp olive oil
500 g/1lb new potatoes, scrubbed
500 g/1lb baby carrots washed and trimmed
salt and pepper

1 To make the stuffing, put the parsnips and carrots into a pan, half cover with water and bring to the boil. Cover the pan and simmer until tender. Drain well then purée in a blender or food processor. Transfer the purée to a bowl and leave to cool.

2 Mix in the breadcrumbs, nutmeg and parsley and season with salt and pepper.

3 Put the stuffing into the neck end of the chicken and push a little under the skin over the breast meat. Secure the flap of skin with a small metal skewer or cocktail stick.

4 Place the bunch of parsley and onion inside the cavity of the chicken, then place the chicken in a large roasting tin.

5 Spread the butter over the skin and season with salt and pepper, cover with foil and place the chicken in a preheated oven, 190°C/375°F/Gas Mark 5, for 30 minutes.

6 Meanwhile, heat the oil in a frying pan, and lightly brown the potatoes.

7 Transfer the potatoes to the roasting tin and add the baby carrots. Baste the chicken and continue to cook for a further hour, basting the chicken and vegetable after 30 minutes.Remove the foil for the last 20 minutes to allow the skin to crisp.

Festive Apple Chicken

The richly flavoured stuffing in this recipe is cooked
under the breast skin of the chicken, so not only is all the flavour sealed in,
but the chicken stays really moist and succulent during cooking.

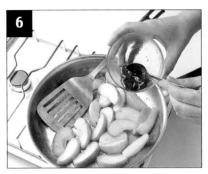

Serves 6
1 chicken, weighing 2 kg/ 4 lb
2 dessert apples
15 g/^{1}/$_2$ oz butter
1 tbsp redcurrant jelly
parsley, to garnish

STUFFING

15 g/^{1}/$_2$ oz butter
1 small onion, chopped finely
60 g/2 oz mushrooms, chopped finely
60 g/2 oz smoked ham, chopped finely
30 g/1 oz fresh breadcrumbs
1 tbsp chopped fresh parsley
1 crisp eating apple
1 tbsp lemon juice
oil, to brush
salt and pepper

1 To make the stuffing, melt the butter and fry the onion gently, stirring until softened but not browned. Stir in the mushrooms and cook over a moderate heat for 2–3 minutes. Remove from the heat and stir in the ham, breadcrumbs and the chopped parsley.

2 Core the apple, leaving the skin on, and grate coarsely. Add the stuffing mixture to the apple with the lemon juice. Season to taste.

3 Loosen the breast skin of the chicken and carefully spoon the stuffing mixture under it, smoothing evenly with your hands.

4 Place the chicken in a roasting tin and brush lightly with oil.

5 Roast the chicken in a preheated oven, 190°C/375°F/Gas Mark 5, for 25 minutes per 500 g/1 lb plus 25 minutes, or until there is no trace of pink in the juices when the chicken is pierced through the thickest part with a skewer. If the breast starts to brown too much, cover the chicken with foil.

6 Core and slice the remaining apples and sauté in the butter until golden. Stir in the redcurrant jelly and warm through until melted. Serve the chicken garnished with the apple slices and parsley.

Chicken with Creamy Courgette & Lime Stuffing

A cheesy stuffing is tucked under the breast skin of the chicken
to give added flavour and moistness to the meat.

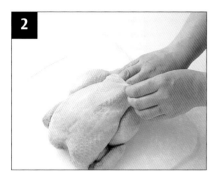

Serves 6

1 chicken, weighing 2.25 kg/5 lb
oil for brushing
250 g/8 oz courgette
30 g/1 oz/2 tbsp butter
juice of 1 lime
lime slices and shreds
of lime rind, to garnish

STUFFING

90 g/3 oz/½ cup courgette
90 g/3 oz medium-fat
soft cheese
finely grated rind of 1 lime
2 tbsp fresh breadcrumbs
salt and pepper

juice until just tender, then serve with
the chicken. Garnish with lime slices
and shreds of lime rind.

COOK'S TIP

For quicker cooking, finely grate the
courgettes rather than cutting them
into strips.

1 To make the stuffing, trim and
coarsely grate the courgette and mix
with the cheese, lime rind,
breadcrumbs, salt and pepper.

2 Carefully ease the skin away from
the breast of the chicken with the
fingertips, taking care not to split it.

3 Push the stuffing under the skin, to
cover the breast evenly.

4 Place in a baking tin, brush with oil
and roast in a preheated oven, 190°C/
375°F/Gas Mark 5, for 20 minutes per
500 g/1 lb plus 20 minutes, or until
the chicken juices run clear when
pierced with a skewer.

5 Meanwhile, trim the remaining
courgettes and cut into long, thin
strips with a potato peeler or sharp
knife. Sauté in the butter and lime

Cheddar Baked Chicken

Cheese and mustard, and a simple, crispy coating, make a delicious
combination for this healthy dish.

Serves 4
1 tbsp milk
2 tbsp prepared English mustard
60 g/2oz grated mature Cheddar cheese
3 tbsp plain flour
2 tbsp chopped fresh chives
4 skinless, boneless chicken breasts

1 Mix together the milk and mustard in a bowl. Mix the cheese with the flour and chives on a plate.

2 Dip the chicken into the milk and mustard mixture, brushing with a pastry brush to coat evenly.

3 Dip the chicken breasts into the cheese mixture, pressing to coat them evenly all over.

4 Place on a baking sheet and spoon any spare cheese coating on top.

5 Bake the chicken in a preheated oven, 200°C/400°F/Gas Mark 6, for 30–35 minutes, or until golden brown and the juices run clear, not pink, when pierced with a skewer. Serve the chicken hot, with jacket potatoes and fresh vegetables, or serve cold, with a crisp salad.

Feta Chicken with Mountain Herbs

Chicken goes well with most savoury herbs, especially during the summer,
when fresh herbs are at their best. This combination makes a good partner
for tangy feta cheese and sun-ripened tomatoes.

Serves 6

8 skinless, boneless chicken thighs

2 tbsp each chopped fresh thyme,
rosemary and oregano

125 g/4 oz feta cheese

salt and pepper

1 tbsp milk

2 tbsp plain flour

salt and pepper

thyme, rosemary and oregano,
to garnish

TOMATO SAUCE

1 medium onion, roughly chopped

1 garlic clove, crushed

1 tbsp olive oil

4 medium plum tomatoes,
quartered

sprig each of thyme, rosemary
and oregano

1 Spread out the chicken thighs on a board, smooth side downwards.

2 Divide the herbs among the chicken thighs, then cut the cheese into eight sticks. Place one stick of cheese in the centre of each chicken thigh. Season well, then roll up to enclose the cheese.

3 Place the rolls in an ovenproof dish, brush with milk and dust with flour to coat evenly.

4 Bake in a preheated oven, 190°C/375°F/Gas Mark 5, for 25–30 minutes, or until golden brown. There should be no pink in the juices when the chicken is pierced with a skewer.

5 To make the sauce, cook the onion and garlic in the olive oil, stirring, until softened and beginning to brown.

6 Add the tomatoes, reduce the heat, cover tightly and simmer gently for 15–20 minutes or until soft.

7 Add the herbs, then transfer to a food processor and blend to a purée. Press through a sieve to make a smooth, rich sauce. Season to taste and serve the sauce with the chicken, garnished with herbs.

Chicken with Baby Onions & Green Peas

Pork fat adds a tasty flavour to this dish. If you can't find fresh garden peas, frozen peas are a good substitute.

Serves 6
250 g/8 oz pork fat, cut into small cubes
60 g/2 oz butter
16 small onions or shallots
1 kg/2 lb boneless chicken pieces
30 g/1 oz plain flour
600 ml/1 pint chicken stock
500 g/1 lb fresh peas
bouquet garni
salt and pepper

1 Place the pork fat cubes in a pan of boiling salted water and simmer for three minutes then drain and dry.

2 Melt the butter in a large frying pan, add the pork and onions, fry gently for 3 minutes until lightly browned.

3 Remove the pork and onions from the pan, add the chicken pieces and brown them all over. Remove them from the pan and transfer the chicken to a baking tray.

4 Add the flour to the pan and cook, stirring until it begins to brown, then slowly blend in the chicken stock.

5 Cook the chicken, with the sauce and bouquet garni, in a preheated oven, 200°C/400°F/Gas Mark 6, for 35 minutes.

6 Remove the bouquet garni about 10 minutes before the end of cooking time and add the onions, pork and peas. Stir to mix.

7 When cooked, place the chicken pieces onto a large platter, surrounded with the pork, peas, onions

COOK'S TIP

If you want to cut down on fat, use lean bacon, cut into small cubes, rather than pork fat.

Golden Chicken with Mango & Cranberries

This recipe, which uses a partly-boned chicken is easy to slice and serve. If you prefer, stuff in the traditional way at the neck end, and cook any remaining stuffing separately.

Serves 6
1 chicken, weighing about 2.25 kg/5 lb
6 slices smoked bacon

STUFFING

1 ripe mango, diced
50g/2oz fresh or frozen cranberries
125 g/4 oz breadcrumbs
$^1/_2$ tsp ground mace
1 egg, beaten
salt and pepper

GLAZE

$^1/_2$ tsp ground turmeric
2 tsp honey
2 tsp sunflower oil
mango slices and cranberries, to garnish

1 To part-bone the chicken, dislocate the legs and place the chicken breast-side downwards.

2 With a sharp knife, cut a straight line through the skin along the ridge of the back.

3 Carefully scrape the meat down from the bone on both sides.

4 When you reach the point where the legs and wings join the body, cut through the joints. Work around the ribcage until the carcass can be lifted away. Make six bacon rolls. Mix the mango with the cranberries, breadcrumbs and mace, then bind with egg. Season with salt and pepper.

5 Place the chicken, skin-side down, and spoon over half the stuffing.

Arrange the bacon rolls down the centre then top with the remaining stuffing. Fold the skin over and tie with string. Turn the chicken over, truss the legs and tuck the wings underneath. Place in a roasting tin. To make the glaze, mix the turmeric, honey and oil and brush over the skin.

6 Roast in a preheated oven, 190°C/375°F/Gas Mark 5, for 1½–2 hours or until the juices run clear, not pink, when the chicken is pierced. Cover loosely with foil once the chicken is browned, to prevent overbrowning. Serve the chicken hot with seasonal vegetables.

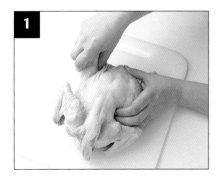

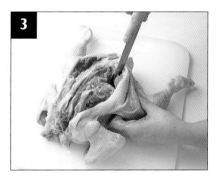

Boned Chicken with Parmesan

It's really very easy to bone a whole chicken, but if you prefer,
you can ask a friendly butcher to do this for you.

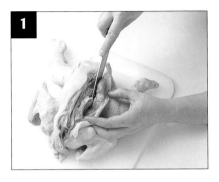

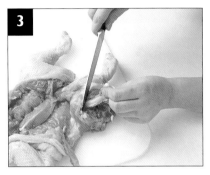

Serves 6

1 chicken, weighing
about 2.25 kg/5 lb

8 slices Mortadella or salami

125 g/4 oz fresh white
or brown breadcrumbs

125 g/4 oz freshly
grated Parmesan cheese

2 garlic cloves, crushed

6 tbsp chopped fresh basil
or parsley

1 egg, beaten

pepper

1 Bone the chicken, keeping the skin intact. Dislocate each leg by breaking it at the thigh joint. Cut down each side of the backbone, taking care not to pierce the breast skin.

2 Pull the backbone clear of the flesh and discard.Remove the ribs, severing any attached flesh with a sharp knife.

3 Scrape away all the flesh from each leg and cut away the bone at the joint with a knife or shears.

4 Use the bones for stock. Lay out the boned chicken on a board, skin side down. Arrange the Mortadella slices over the chicken, overlapping slightly.

5 Combine the breadcrumbs, Parmesan, garlic and basil, season well with pepper and stir in the beaten egg to bind. Pile the mixture down the middle of the boned chicken, roll the meat around it and tie securely with fine cotton string.

6 Place in a roasting dish and brush lightly with olive oil. Roast in a preheated oven, 200°C/400°F/Gas Mark 6, for 1½ hours or until the juices run clear when pierced.

7 Serve hot or cold, in slices, with fresh spring vegetables.

Casseroles

Long, slow cooking means meltingly succulent meat with a good, rich flavour. Because chicken itself does not have a strong flavour, it marries happily with almost any other ingredient and the recipes in this section exploit that quality. They are drawn from many cuisines from around the world, and there are dishes from Italy, France, Hungary, Asia, the Caribbean, and from the USA. French classics include Coq au Vin Blanc, Garlic Chicken Cassoulet, Bourguignonne of Chicken, and

Chicken with 40 Garlic Cloves, a recipe that is not as daunting as it sounds. After cooking, the garlic becomes surprisingly mild and sweet. Chicken also makes a good partner for olives, beans and rice, and pilaus and jambalayas are just some of the dishes on offer. Spicy Cajun recipes include Chicken Etouffé and Grillades with Grits.

Chicken Cacciatore

This is a popular Italian classic in which browned chicken quarters
are cooked in a richly flavoured sauce of tomatoes and peppers.

Serves 4

1 roasting chicken, weighing
1.5 kg/3 lb, cut into
6 or 8 serving pieces

120 g/4 oz plain flour

3 tbsp olive oil

150 ml/$^1/_4$ pt/$^2/_3$ cup dry white wine

1 green pepper, sliced

1 red pepper, sliced

1 carrot, chopped finely

1 celery stick, chopped finely

1 garlic clove, crushed

200 g/7 oz can of chopped
tomatoes

salt and pepper

1 Rinse and pat dry the chicken pieces.

2 Lightly dust them with seasoned
flour and brown them over a medium
heat in the olive oil. When browned
all over, set the pieces aside.

3 Drain off all but 2 tablespoons of
the fat in the pan, add the wine and
stir for a few minutes. Add the
peppers, carrot, celery and garlic,
season well and simmer together for
about 15 minutes.

4 Add the chopped tomatoes and the
chicken pieces to the pan. Cover and
simmer for 30 minutes, stirring often,
until the chicken is cooked.

5 Check the seasoning before serving
piping hot.

Chicken with 40 Garlic Cloves

In France, the chicken is served accompanied by slices of bread. Each diner
spreads the bread with the softened and sweetened garlic.

Serves 4
1 roasting chicken, weighing about 1.5 kg/ 3 lb
15 g/^{1}/$_2$ oz fresh thyme
15 g/^{1}/$_2$ oz fresh rosemary
15 g/^{1}/$_2$ oz fresh sage
15 g/^{1}/$_2$ oz fresh parsley
2 small celery sticks
40 fresh garlic cloves, unpeeled
4 tbsp olive oil
salt and pepper

1 Wash and pat dry the chicken and rub salt into the skin.

2 Stuff the cavity with half of the fresh herbs, celery, and 10 of the garlic cloves.

3 Place the chicken in a roasting tin or earthenware dish, arrange the rest of the herbs, celery and garlic around the chicken, and smear oil all over the skin.

4 Roast in a preheated oven, 200°C/400°F/Gas Mark 6, for 1½ hours, basting frequently.

5 Transfer the cooked chicken to a warmed serving platter, and surround with the cloves of garlic. Skim most of the fat from the cooking juices, bring to the boil in the pan, and reduce slightly. Strain into a warmed sauce boat to serve.

Chicken & Chilli Bean Pot

This Mexican aromatic chicken dish has a spicy kick. Chicken thighs are not only more economical than breasts, they have much more flavour when cooked in this way.

Serves 4
2 tbsp plain flour
1 tsp chilli powder
8 chicken thighs or
4 chicken legs
3 tbsp olive or vegetable oil
2 garlic cloves, crushed
1 large onion, chopped
1 green or red pepper,
chopped
300 ml/$^1/_2$ pint
chicken stock
2 medium tomatoes, chopped
425 g/14 oz can of red kidney
beans, rinsed and drained
2 tbsp tomato purée
salt and pepper

5 Return the chicken to the pan. Reduce the heat and simmer, covered, for about 30 minutes, until the chicken is tender. Season with salt and pepper to taste. Transfer to a warm serving dish and serve at once.

1 Mix together the flour, chilli powder, and salt and pepper in a shallow dish. Rinse the chicken, but do not dry. Dip the chicken into the seasoned flour, coating it on all sides.

2 Heat the oil in a large, deep frying pan or saucepan and add the chicken. Cook over a high heat for 3–4 minutes, turning the pieces to brown them all over. Remove with a perforated spoon and drain on absorbent paper towels.

3 Add the garlic, onion and pepper to the pan and fry gently for 2–3 minutes until softened.

4 Add the stock, tomatoes, kidney beans and tomato purée, stirring well. Bring to the boil.

COOK'S TIP

Serve this spicy dish with boiled rice or warmed tortillas, with a side dish of soured cream or natural yogurt.

Chicken with Green Olives

Olives are a popular flavouring for poultry and game in Apulia in Italy, where this recipe originates. In Italy every bit of the bird is used in some way, most often for soups and stock.

Serves 4
4 chicken breasts, part boned
2 tbsp olive oil
30 g/1 oz butter
1 large onion, chopped finely
2 garlic cloves, crushed
2 red, yellow or green peppers, cut into large pieces
250 g/8 oz large closed-cup mushrooms, sliced or quartered
2 small tomatoes, peeled and halved
150 ml/¼ pint dry white wine
125 g/4 oz green olives, pitted
4–6 tbsp double cream
salt and pepper
chopped flat-leafed parsley, to garnish
pasta or tiny new potatoes, to serve

1 Season the chicken with salt and pepper. Heat the oil and butter in a frying pan, add the chicken and fry until browned all over. Remove from the pan and keep warm.

2 Add the onion and garlic to the pan and fry gently until beginning to soften. Add the peppers and the mushrooms and continue to cook for a few minutes longer.

3 Add the tomatoes and plenty of seasoning to the pan, and then transfer the vegetable mixture to an ovenproof casserole. Place the chicken on the bed of vegetables.

4 Add the wine to the pan and bring to the boil. Pour the wine over the chicken and cover the casserole. Cook in a preheated oven, 180°C/350°F/Gas Mark 4, for 50 minutes.

5 Add the olives to the chicken, mix lightly then pour on the cream. Re-cover the casserole and return to the oven for 10–20 minutes or until the chicken is very tender.

6 Adjust the seasoning and serve the pieces of chicken, surrounded by the vegetables and sauce, with pasta or tiny new potatoes. Sprinkle with parsley to garnish.

Roman Chicken

This Roman dish is equally good cold and could be taken on a picnic
– serve with bread to mop up the juices.

Serves 4
4 tbsp olive oil
6 chicken pieces
4 large mixed red, green and yellow peppers
1 large red onion, sliced
2 garlic cloves, crushed with 1 tsp salt
125 g/4 oz pitted green olives
Tomato Sauce (page 124)
300 ml/½ pint hot chicken stock
2 sprigs fresh marjoram
salt and pepper

1 Heat half the oil in a flameproof casserole and brown the chicken pieces on all sides. Remove the chicken pieces and set aside.

2 Remove the seeds and the cores from the pepper and cut them into strips.

3 Add the remaining oil to the casserole. Fry the onion gently for 5–7 minutes until just softened, then add the garlic and fry for another minute. Stir in the peppers, olives and tomato sauce and bring to the boil.

4 Return the chicken to the casserole with the stock and the marjoram. Cover the casserole and simmer for about 45 minutes until the chicken is tender. Season to taste with salt and pepper and serve with crusty bread.

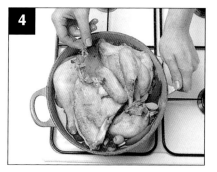

Coq au Vin Blanc

Small pieces of chicken are gently simmered with wine, herbs, bacon, mushrooms
and onions to produce a dish reminiscent of an authentic French meal.

Serves 2
2 chicken leg quarters
4 thick lean back bacon slices, derinded
2 tbsp oil
8 button onions or 1 large onion, sliced
1 garlic clove, crushed
150 ml/¼ pint dry white wine
300 ml/½ pint chicken stock
1 bay leaf
large pinch of dried oregano
1 tbsp cornflour
60 g/2 oz/¾ cup tiny button mushrooms, trimmed
salt and pepper
chopped fresh parsley, to garnish
boiled rice or creamed potatoes, to serve

1 Cut each chicken leg into two pieces and season well with salt and pepper. Cut the bacon into 1 cm/½ inch strips.

2 Heat the oil in a saucepan. Fry the chicken until golden brown and remove from the pan. Add the bacon, onions and garlic, and fry until browned. Drain the fat from the pan.

3 Add the wine, stock, bay leaf, oregano, and salt and pepper to the saucepan. Return the chicken to the pan and bring to the boil.

4 Cover the saucepan tightly and simmer very gently for about 40–50 minutes, or until the chicken is tender and cooked through and the juices run clear when pierced with a skewer.

5 Blend the cornflour with a little cold water and add to the saucepan with the mushrooms. Bring back to the boil and simmer for a further 5 minutes.

6 Adjust the seasoning and discard the bay leaf. Serve sprinkled liberally with chopped parsley, and with boiled rice or creamed potatoes.

Country Chicken Casserole

Most ceramic casserole dishes can be used with care on the hob, but a diffuser can be placed between the heat and the dish – it is usually a double layer of perforated metal holding the dish off the heat. However, you can simply sauté the chicken then transfer it to an ovenproof dish.

Serves 4
1 free-range chicken, 1.5 kg/ 3 lb, cut into pieces
flour for dusting
30 g/1 oz butter
1 tsp olive oil
10 pickling onions
3 cloves garlic, unpeeled
1 carrot, diced
1 celery stick, diced
1 bay leaf
125 g/4 oz smoked streaky bacon, diced
600 ml/1 pint stock, or to cover
750 g/1¹/₂ lb waxy potatoes, sliced
salt and pepper

1 Rinse and pat dry the chicken pieces. Dust with flour. Melt the butter with the oil over medium-high heat and brown the chicken pieces well all over. Set aside.

2 Add the onions, garlic, carrot, celery, bay leaf and bacon to the pan. Cook over a medium heat for 10 minutes, and season well. Return the chicken to the pan and pour on the stock. Check the seasoning.

3 Arrange the sliced potatoes over the top of the casserole. Cover and simmer for 1 hour.

4 Serve piping hot with a selection of green vegetables.

Chicken & Vegetable Rice

Boneless chicken breasts may be used instead of the drumsticks, in which case
slash them diagonally to allow the flavours of the sauce to penetrate.

Serves 4–6
4 chicken drumsticks
3 tbsp mango chutney
1$\frac{1}{2}$ tbsp lemon juice
6 tbsp vegetable oil
1–2 tbsp medium or hot curry paste
1$\frac{1}{2}$ tsp paprika
1 large onion, chopped
125 g/4 oz button mushrooms
2 carrots, sliced thinly
2 celery sticks, trimmed and sliced thinly
$\frac{1}{2}$ aubergine, quartered and sliced
2 garlic cloves, crushed
$\frac{1}{2}$ tsp ground cinnamon
250 g/8 oz long-grain rice
600 ml/1 pint chicken stock or water
60 g/2 oz frozen peas or sliced French green beans
60 g/2 oz seedless raisins
salt and pepper
wedges of hard-boiled egg and lemon slices, to garnish

1 Slash the drumsticks twice on each side, cutting through the skin and deep into the flesh. Mix the chutney with the lemon juice, 1 tablespoon of the oil, the curry paste and paprika. Brush over the drumsticks and reserve the remainder.

2 Heat 2 tablespoons of oil in the frying pan and fry the drumsticks for about 5 minutes until sealed and golden brown all over.

3 Meanwhile, heat the remaining oil. Add the onion, mushrooms, carrots, celery, aubergine, garlic and cinnamon, and fry for 1 minute. Stir in the rice and cook for 1 minute. Stir to coat the rice with the oil. Add the stock and the remaining mango chutney mixture, peas and raisins. Mix and bring to the boil.

4 Reduce the heat and add the drumsticks to the mixture, pushing them down into the liquid. Cover and cook gently for 25 minutes until the liquid is absorbed, the drumsticks are tender and the rice is cooked.

5 Transfer the rice to a warmed serving plate and arrange the drumsticks around it. Garnish the dish with wedges of hard-boiled egg and lemon slices, if using.

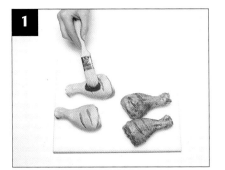

Jambalaya

Jambalaya, New Orlean's paella, dates back to the 18th century, when it was served as slave food. Today, this hearty rice dish can contain any number of meats, such as chicken, duck, ham or sausage.

Serves 4
60 g/2 oz butter
2 onions, chopped
2 garlic cloves, crushed
5 celery sticks, chopped
1 red pepper, chopped
1 green pepper, chopped
1 tsp Cajun Spice Mixture (page 175)
250 g/8 oz long-grain rice
425 g/14 oz can of tomatoes, drained and chopped
500 g/1 lb cooked assorted meats (chicken, duck, ham or sausage), sliced or diced
250 ml/8 fl oz vegetable stock or white wine
1 tsp salt
parsley sprigs, to garnish

1 Melt the butter in a large, heavy-based pan. Add the onions, garlic, celery, peppers and spice mixture and mix well.

2 Add the rice and stir well to coat the grains in the butter mixture.

3 Add the tomatoes, meats, stock or wine and salt. Bring to the boil, stirring well.

4 Reduce the heat, cover and simmer for about 15 minutes or until the rice is cooked and fluffy and has absorbed all the liquid. If the mixture seems to be too dry then add a little boiling water, tablespoon by tablespoon, towards the end of the cooking time.

5 Serve the jamabalaya on warm plates, garnished with parsley.

Baton Rouge Chicken Gumbo

Everyone in the state of Louisiana, USA, has their own favourite gumbo recipe.
This one uses chicken with prawns, okra and a little belly of pork:
a recipe that is hard to improve upon.

Serves 4–6
30 g/1 oz butter
1 tbsp corn oil
30 g/1 oz plain flour
90 g/3 oz belly pork, sliced
1 large onion, sliced
2 celery sticks, chopped
500 g/1 lb okra, trimmed and sliced
425 g/14 oz can peeled tomatoes
2 garlic cloves, crushed
1 litre/1³/₄ pints chicken stock or water
250 g/8 oz peeled prawns
500 g/1 lb cooked chicken, skinned and cut into bite-sized pieces
1 tsp Tabasco sauce
500 g/1 lb hot cooked rice, to serve

1 Heat the butter and oil in a small, heavy-based pan. Add the flour and cook, stirring frequently, over a low heat until the roux turns a rich brown colour. Set aside.

2 Meanwhile, in a large pan, fry the pork slices gently, without extra fat, until they are golden brown on all sides and the fat has been rendered. Add the sliced onion and celery, and cook for a further 5 minutes.

3 Stir in the okra and fry gently for a further 3 minutes. Stir in the tomatoes and garlic, and simmer over gentle heat for 15 minutes.

4 Gradually add the stock to the browned roux, mixing and blending well, then add to the okra mixture. Cover and simmer for 1 hour.

5 Add the prawns and chicken to the okra mixture, cook for a further 5 minutes until the chicken is thoroughly reheated. Stir in the Tabasco.

6 Spoon the gumbo into individual serving bowls and top with a scoop of hot cooked rice.

Chicken Etouffé

Etouffé means smothered and is a popular way of presenting food in Cajun cuisine. Here, strips of chicken and vegetables are smothered in a thickened dark sauce flavoured with basil.

Serves 4–6
60 g/2 oz butter
1 small onion, chopped
1 celery stick, chopped
1 small green pepper, chopped
1 red pepper, cored, chopped
1 small red chilli, deseeded and finely chopped
1 tsp Cajun Spice Mixture (page 175)
1 tsp chopped fresh basil
2 tbsp vegetable oil
2 tbsp flour
475 ml/16 fl oz rich chicken stock
500 g/1 lb skinless, boneless chicken breasts, cut into strips or bite-sized pieces
4 spring onions, chopped
salt
rice or couscous, to serve

1 Melt the butter in a large, heavy-based pan. Add the onion, celery, green and red peppers and chilli and cook over a gentle heat until softened, about 5 minutes.

2 Add the Cajun Spice Mixture, basil and salt. Cook for a further 2 minutes.

3 Meanwhile, heat the oil in a pan, add the flour and cook, slowly, until a rich red/brown roux is formed. Whisk constantly to prevent the roux from scorching and becoming bitter.

4 Gradually add the stock and whisk well to make a smooth thickened sauce. Pour the sauce over the vegetable mixture and allow to simmer for about 15 minutes.

5 Add the chicken strips and the spring onions and cook for a further 10 minutes, stirring occasionally until the chicken is cooked and tender.

6 Serve with cooked long-grain rice or freshly cooked fluffy couscous.

Grillades with Grits

Grillades is a Cajun meat and vegetable stew in a thick gravy. It is considered to be
Bayou breakfast food and would always be served with grits, a kind of creamy
cereal (not unlike porridge) made from corn.

Serves 6
4 tbsp olive oil
1 kg/2 lb skinless, boneless chicken breasts, cut into 7 × 10 cm/3 × 4 inch strips
60 g/2 oz/$^1/_2$ cup plain flour
3 onions, chopped
2 green peppers, chopped
4 celery sticks, finely chopped
1 garlic clove, crushed
3 medium ripe tomatoes, peeled, deseeded and chopped
2 tbsp tomato purée
1 tsp chopped fresh thyme
$^1/_2$–1 tsp Tabasco sauce
$1^1/_2$ tsp paprika
$^1/_4$ tsp cayenne pepper
1 tsp salt
150 ml/1$^1/_4$ pint vegetable stock
150 ml/$^1/_4$ pint white wine
grits hominy or couscous, to serve

1 Heat the oil in a heavy-based frying pan. Add the chicken strips and fry quickly on both sides until no longer pink and they are sealed all over. Remove with perforated spoon and set aside.

2 Add the flour to the pan juices and mix well, stirring until the flour is absorbed by the juices. Cook over a gentle heat, stirring constantly, until the roux changes to a rich brown colour.

3 Add the onions, peppers, celery and garlic, and mix. Cover and cook over a gentle heat for 15 minutes.

4 Return the meat to the pan with the tomatoes, tomato purée, thyme, Tabasco sauce, paprika, cayenne, salt, stock and wine, mixing well.

5 Cover and simmer gently for a further 40–45 minutes, or until the chicken and vegetables are cooked.

6 Serve hot with grits or couscous.

Bourguignonne of Chicken

A recipe based on a classic French dish. Use a good quality wine
when making this casserole.

Serves 4–6
4 tbsp sunflower oil
900 g/1³/₄ lb chicken meat, diced
250 g/8 oz button mushrooms
125 g/4 oz rindless, smoked bacon, diced
16 shallots
2 garlic cloves, crushed
1 tbsp plain flour
150ml/¹/₄ pint white Burgundy wine
150ml/¹/₄ pint chicken stock
1 bouquet garni (1 bay leaf, sprig thyme, stick of celery, parsley and sage tied with string)
salt and pepper

1 Heat the sunflower oil in an ovenproof casserole and brown the chicken all over, remove from the casserole with a slotted spoon.

2 Add the mushrooms, bacon, shallots and garlic to the casserole and cook for 4 minutes.

3 Return the chicken to the casserole and sprinkle with flour. Cook for a further 2 minutes.

4 Add the wine and stock and stir until boiling. Add the bouquet garni and season well with salt and pepper.

5 Cover the casserole and bake in the centre of a preheated oven, 150°C/300°F/Gas Mark 2, for 1½ hours. Remove the bouquet garni.

6 Deep fry some heart-shaped croûtons (about 8 large ones) in beef dripping and serve with the bourguignonne.

COOK'S TIP

A good quality red wine can be used instead of the white wine, to produce a rich, glossy red sauce.

Spiced Chicken Casserole

Spices, herbs, fruit, nuts and vegetables are combined to make an appealing casserole with lots of flavour.

Serves 4–6
3 tbsp olive oil
900 g/1³/₄ lb chicken meat, sliced
10 shallots or pickling onions
3 carrots, chopped
60 g/2 ozchestnuts, sliced
60 g/2 oz flaked almonds, toasted
1 tsp freshly grated nutmeg
3 tsp ground cinnamon
300 ml/¹/₂ pint white wine
300 ml/¹/₂ pint chicken stock
175 ml/ 6fl oz white wine vinegar
1 tbsp chopped fresh tarragon
1 tbsp chopped fresh flat leaf parsley
1 tbsp chopped fresh thyme
grated rind of 1 orange
1 tbsp dark muscovado sugar
125 g/4 oz
seedless black grapes, halved
sea salt and pepper
fresh herbs, to garnish

1 Heat the olive oil in a large saucepan and fry the chicken, shallots and carrots for about 6 minutes until browned.

2 Add the remaining ingredients, except the grapes, and simmer over a low heat for 2 hours until the meat is very tender.

3 Add the grapes just before serving and serve with wild rice or puréed potato. Garnish with herbs.

Hungarian Chicken Goulash

Goulash is traditionally made with beef, but this recipe successfully uses chicken instead.
To reduce fat, use a low-fat cream in place of the soured cream.

Serves 6
900 g/1¾ lb chicken meat, diced
60 g/2 oz flour, seasoned with
1 tsp paprika, salt and pepper
2 tbsp olive oil
30 g/1 oz butter
1 onion, sliced
24 shallots, peeled
1 each red and green pepper, chopped
1 tbsp paprika
1 tsp rosemary, crushed
4 tbsp tomato purée
300 ml/½ pint chicken stock
150 ml/¼ pint claret
425 g/14 oz can chopped tomatoes
150ml/¼ pint soured cream
1 tbsp chopped fresh parsley, to garnish

1 Toss the meat into the seasoned flour until coated all over.

2 In a flameproof casserole, heat the oil and butter and fry the onion, shallots and peppers for 3 minutes.

3 Add the chicken and cook for a further 4 minutes.

4 Sprinkle with the paprika and rosemary.

5 Add the tomato purée, chicken stock, claret and chopped tomatoes, cover and cook in the centre of a preheated oven, 160°C/325°F/Gas Mark 3 for 1½ hours.

6 Remove the casserole from the oven, allow it to stand for 4 minutes, then add the soured cream and garnish with parsley.

7 Serve with chunks of bread and a side salad.

COOK'S VARIATION

Serve the goulash with buttered ribbon noodles instead of bread. For an authentic touch, try a Hungarian red wine instead of the claret.

Chicken with Shallots in Wild Mushroom & Ginger Sauce

This recipe has an oriental flavour, which can be further enhanced
with chopped spring onions, cinnamon and lemon grass.

Serves 6–8
6 tbsp sesame oil
900 g/1¾ lb chicken meat
60 g/2 oz flour, seasoned
32 shallots, sliced
500 g/1 lb wild mushrooms, roughly chopped
300 ml/½ pint chicken stock
2 tbsp Worcestershire sauce
1 tbsp honey
2 tbsp grated fresh root ginger
150 ml/¼ pint yogurt
salt and pepper
flat leaf parsley, to garnish

1 Heat the oil in a large frying pan. Coat the chicken in the seasoned flour and cook for about 4 minutes, until browned all over. Transfer to a large deep casserole.

2 Slowly fry the shallots and mushrooms in the juices.

3 Add the chicken stock, Worcestershire sauce, honey and fresh ginger, then season to taste with salt and pepper.

4 Pour the mixture over the chicken, and cover the casserole with a lid or cooking foil.

5 Cook in the centre of a preheated oven, 150°C/300°F/Gas Mark 2, for 1½ hours until the meat is very tender. Add the yogurt and cook for a further 10 minutes. Serve with a mixture of wild rice and white rice, and garnish with parsley.

Fricasseé of Chicken in Lime Sauce

The addition of lime juice and lime rind adds a delicious tangy
flavour to this chicken stew.

Serves 4
2 tbsp oil
1 large chicken, cut into small portions
60 g/2 oz flour, seasoned
500 g/1 lb baby onions or shallots, sliced
1 each green and red pepper, sliced thinly
150 ml/¼ pint chicken stock
juice and rind of 2 limes
2 chillies, chopped
2 tbsp oyster sauce
1 tsp Worcestershire sauce
salt and pepper

1 Heat the oil in a large frying pan. Coat the chicken pieces in the seasoned flour and cook for about 4 minutes until browned all over.

2 Transfer the chicken to a large, deep casserole and sprinkle with the sliced onions.

3 Slowly fry the peppers in the juices in the frying pan.

4 Add the chicken stock, lime juice and rind and cook for a further 5 minutes.

5 Add the chillies, oyster sauce and Worcestershire sauce. Season to taste.

6 Pour the peppers and juices over the chicken and onions.

7 Cover the casserole with a lid or cooking foil.

8 Cook in the centre of a preheated oven, 190°C/375°F/Gas Mark 5, for 1½ hours until the chicken is very tender, then serve.

COOK'S TIP

Try this casserole with a cheese scone topping. About 30 minutes before the end of cooking time, simply top with rounds cut from cheese scone pastry.

Brittany Chicken Casserole

A hearty, one-dish meal that would make a substantial lunch or supper.

Serves 6
500 g/1 lb beans, such as flageolets, soaked overnight and drained
30 g/1 oz butter
2 tbsp olive oil
3 rindless bacon slices, chopped
900 g/1¾ lb chicken pieces
1 tbsp plain flour
300 ml/½ pint cider
150 ml/¼ pint chicken stock
14 shallots
2 tbsp honey, warmed
250 g/8 oz ready-cooked beetroot
salt and pepper

1 Cook the beans in salted boiling water for about 25 minutes.

2 Heat the butter and olive oil in a flameproof casserole, add the bacon and chicken and cook for 5 minutes.

3 Sprinkle with flour then add the cider and chicken stock. Mix well, season and bring to the boil.

4 Add the beans, cover tightly with a lid or cooking foil and bake in the centre of a preheated oven, 160°C/325°F/Gas Mark 3, for 2 hours.

5 About 15 minutes before the end of cooking time, remove the lid or cooking foil from the casserole.

6 Gently cook the shallots and honey together in a frying for 5 minutes.

7 Add the shallots and cooked beetroot to the casserole and leave to finish cooking in the oven for the last 15 minutes.

COOK'S TIP

To save time, use canned flageolet beans instead of dried. Drain and rinse before adding to the chicken.

Chicken Madeira "French-style"

Madeira adds a rich, full flavour to this casserole dish.

Serves 8
30 g/1 oz butter
20 baby onions
280 g/9 oz carrots, sliced
280 g/9 oz bacon, chopped
280 g/9 oz button mushrooms
1 chicken, weighing about 1.5 kg/3 lb
425 ml/15 fl oz white wine
30 g/1 oz seasoned flour
425ml/15 fl oz chicken stock
bouquet garni
150 ml/$\frac{1}{4}$ pint Madeira wine
salt and pepper

1 Heat the butter in a large frying pan and fry the onions, carrots, bacon and mushrooms for 3 minutes. Transfer to a large casserole dish.

2 Add the chicken to the frying pan and brown all over. Transfer to the casserole dish with the vegetables and bacon.

3 Add the wine and cook until the wine is nearly completely reduced.

4 Sprinkle with the seasoned flour.

5 Add the chicken stock, salt and pepper and the bouquet garni. Cover and cook for 2 hours. About 30 minutes before the end of cooking time, add the Madeira and cook uncovered.

6 Carve the chicken and serve with mashed potato or pasta.

Garlic Chicken Cassoulet

This is a cassoulet with a twist – it is made with chicken instead of duck and lamb.
Save time by using canned beans, such as borlotti or cannellini beans,
which are both good in this dish.

Serves 4
4 tbsp sunflower oil
900 g/1³/₄ lb chicken meat, chopped
250 g/8 oz mushrooms, sliced
16 shallots
6 garlic cloves, crushed
1 tbsp plain flour
250 ml/8 fl oz white wine
250 ml/8 fl oz chicken stock
1 bouquet garni (1 bay leaf, sprig thyme, celery, parsley & sage tied with string)
425 g/14 oz can borlotti beans
salt and pepper

1 Heat the sunflower oil in an ovenproof casserole and fry the chicken until browned all over. Remove from the casserole with a slotted spoon.

2 Add the mushrooms, shallots and garlic to the fat in the casserole and cook for 4 minutes.

3 Return the chicken to the casserole and sprinkle with the flour then cook for a further 2 minutes.

4 Add the wine and stock, stir until boiling then add the bouquet garni. Season well with salt and pepper.

5 Stir in the borlotti beans.

6 Cover and place in the centre of a preheated oven, 150°C/300°F/Gas Mark 2, for 2 hours. Remove the bouquet garni and serve.

Country Chicken Braise with Rosemary Dumplings

Root vegetables are always cheap and nutritious, and combined with chicken they make tasty and economical casseroles.

Serves 4
4 chicken quarters
2 tbsp sunflower oil
2 medium leeks
250 g/8 oz carrots, chopped
250 g/8 oz parsnips, chopped
2 small turnips, chopped
600 ml/1 pint chicken stock
3 tbsp Worcestershire sauce
2 sprigs fresh rosemary
salt and pepper

DUMPLINGS

200 g/7 oz self-raising flour
105 g/3¹/₂ oz shredded suet
1 tbsp chopped rosemary leaves
cold water, to mix

1 Remove the skin from the chicken if you prefer. Heat the oil in a large, flameproof casserole or heavy pan and fry the chicken until golden. Remove from the pan. Drain off the excess fat.

2 Trim and slice the leeks. Add the carrots, parsnips and turnips to the casserole and cook for 5 minutes, until lightly coloured. Return the chicken to the pan.

3 Add the stock, Worcestershire sauce, rosemary and seasoning, then bring to the boil.

4 Reduce the heat, cover and simmer gently for about 50 minutes or until the chicken juices run clear when the chicken is pierced with a skewer.

5 To make the dumplings, combine the flour, suet and rosemary leaves with salt and pepper in a bowl. Stir in just enough cold water to bind to a firm dough.

6 Form into eight small balls and place on top of the chicken and vegetables. Cover and simmer for a further 10–12 minutes, until the dumplings are well risen.

Rustic Chicken & Orange Pot

Low in fat and high in fibre, this colourful casserole
makes a healthy and hearty meal.

Serves 4

8 chicken drumsticks, skinned

1 tbsp wholemeal flour

1 tbsp olive oil

2 medium red onions

1 garlic clove, crushed

1 tsp fennel seeds

1 bay leaf

finely grated rind and juice
of 1 small orange

425 g/14 oz can chopped
tomatoes

425 g/14 oz can cannellini
or flageolet beans, drained

salt and black pepper

TOPPING

3 thick slices wholemeal
bread

2 tsp olive oil

1 Toss the chicken drumsticks in the flour to coat evenly. Heat the oil in a non-stick or heavy pan and fry the chicken over a fairly high heat, turning often until golden brown. Transfer to a large ovenproof casserole.

2 Slice the red onions into thin wedges. Add to the pan and cook for a few minutes until lightly browned. Stir in the garlic, then add the onions and garlic to the casserole.

3 Add the fennel seeds, bay leaf, orange rind and juice, tomatoes, beans and salt and pepper.

4 Cover tightly and cook in a preheated oven, 190°C/375°F/Gas Mark 5, for 30–35 minutes until the chicken juices are clear and not pink when pierced through the thickest part with a skewer.

5 For the topping, cut the bread into small dice and toss in the oil. Remove the lid from the casserole and top with the bread cubes. Bake for a further 15–20 minutes until the bread is golden and crisp. Serve hot.

Old English Chicken Stewed in Ale

A slow-cooked, old-fashioned stew to warm up a wintry day.
The rarebit toasts are a perfect accompaniment to soak up the rich juices,
but if you prefer, serve the stew with jacket potatoes.

Serves 4–6

4 large, skinless chicken thighs
2 tbsp plain flour
2 tbsp English mustard powder
2 tbsp sunflower oil
15 g/$\frac{1}{2}$ oz butter
4 small onions
600 ml/1 pint beer
2 tbsp Worcestershire sauce
3 tbsp chopped fresh sage leaves
salt and pepper

FOR THE RAREBIT TOASTS

60 g/2 oz grated mature
English Cheddar
1 tsp English mustard powder
1 tsp plain flour
1 tsp Worcestershire sauce
1 tbsp beer
2 slices wholemeal toast

1 Trim any excess fat from the chcken and toss in the flour and mustard to coat evenly. Heat the oil and butter in a large flameproof casserole and fry the chicken over a fairly high heat, turning occasionally until golden. Remove and keep hot.

2 Peel and slice the onions into wedges and fry quickly until golden. Add the chicken, beer, Worcestershire sauce, and salt and pepper. Bring to the boil, cover and simmer very gently for about 1½ hours, until the chicken is very tender.

3 Meanwhile, make the rarebit toasts: mix the cheese with the mustard, flour, Worcestershire sauce

and beer. Spread over the toasts and place under a hot grill for about 1 minute, until melted and golden. Cut into triangles.

4 Stir the sage into the chicken stew, bring to the boil and serve with the rarebit toasts, a green vegetable and new potatoes.

Jamaican Hot Pot

A tasty way to make chicken joints go a long way, this hearty casserole, spiced with the warm, subtle flavour of ginger, is a good choice for a Halloween party. If squash or pumpkin is not available, swede makes a good substitute.

Serves 4
2 tsp sunflower oil
4 chicken drumsticks
4 chicken thighs
1 medium onion
750 g/1^1/$_2$ lb piece squash or pumpkin, diced
1 green pepper, sliced
2.5 cm/1 inch fresh ginger root, chopped finely
425 g/14 oz can chopped tomatoes
300ml/^{1}/$_2$ pint chicken stock
60 g/2 oz split lentils
garlic salt and cayenne pepper
350 g/12 oz can sweetcorn

1 Heat the oil in a large flameproof casserole and fry the chicken joints until golden, turning frequently.

2 Peel and slice the onion.

3 Peel and slice the squash or pumpkin.

4 Deseed and slice the pepper.

5 Drain excess fat from the pan and add the onion, pumpkin and pepper. Gently fry for a few minutes until lightly browned. Add the ginger, tomatoes, stock and lentils. Season lightly with garlic salt and cayenne.

6 Cover and place in a preheated oven, 190°C/375°F/Gas Mark 5, for about 1 hour, until the vegetables are

tender and the juices from the chicken run clear. Add the drained corn and cook for a further 5 minutes. Season to taste and serve with crusty bread.

COOK'S VARIATION

If you can't find fresh ginger root, add 1 teaspoon allspice for a warm, fragrant aroma.

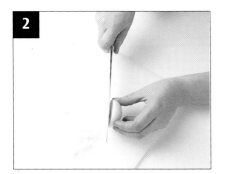

Springtime Chicken Cobbler

Fresh spring vegetables are the basis of this colourful casserole, which is topped with hearty wholemeal dumplings for a complete, healthy family meal. Vary the vegetables depending on what's available.

Serves 4
8 skinless chicken drumsticks
1 tbsp oil
1 small onion, sliced
350 g/12 oz baby carrots
2 baby turnips
125 g/4 oz broad beans or peas
1 tsp cornflour
300ml/½ pint chicken stock
2 bay leaves
salt and pepper

COBBLER TOPPING

250 g/8 oz/2 cups wholemeal plain flour
2 tsp baking powder
30 g/1 oz sunflower soft margarine
2 tsp dry wholegrain mustard
60 g/2 oz Cheddar cheese, grated
skimmed milk, to mix
sesame seeds, to sprinkle

1 Fry the chicken in the oil, turning, until golden brown. Drain well and place in an ovenproof casserole. Sauté the onion for 2–3 minutes to soften.

2 Wash and trim the carrots and turnips and cut into equal-sized pieces. Add to the casserole with the onions and beans or peas.

3 Blend the cornflour with a little of the stock, then stir in the rest and heat gently, stirring until boiling. Pour into the casserole and add the bay leaves, salt and pepper.

4 Cover tightly and bake in a preheated oven, 200°C/400°F/Gas

Mark 6, for 50–60 minutes, or until the chicken juices run clear when pierced with a skewer.

5 For the topping, sift the flour and baking powder. Mix in the margarine with a fork. Stir in the mustard, the cheese and enough milk to mix to a fairly soft dough.

6 Roll out and cut 16 rounds with a 4 cm/1½ inch cutter.Uncover the casserole, arrange the scone rounds on top, then brush with milk and sprinkle with sesame seeds. Bake in the oven for 20 minutes or until the topping is golden and firm.

Country Chicken Bake

This economical bake is a complete meal to cook and serve in one pot – and it's easy to adjust for any amount of servings. Its crusty, herb-flavoured French bread topping mops up the tasty juices, and means there's no need to serve potatoes or rice separately.

Serves 4
2 tbsp sunflower oil
4 chicken quarters
16 small whole onions, peeled
3 sticks celery, sliced
425 g/14 oz can red kidney beans
4 medium tomatoes, quartered
200 ml/7floz
dry cider or stock
4 tbsp chopped fresh parsley
1 tsp paprika
60 g/2 oz butter
12 slices French bread
salt and pepper

1 Heat the oil in a flameproof casserole and fry the chicken quarters two at a time until golden. Remove from the pan and set aside.

2 Add the onions, turning occasionally, until golden brown. Add the celery and fry for 2–3 minutes, then stir in the beans, tomatoes, cider, half the parsley, salt and pepper. Sprinkle with the paprika.

3 Return the chicken to the pan and stir in the beans, tomatoes, cider, half the parsley and salt and pepper. Sprinkle with the paprika. Cover and cook in a preheated oven, 200°C/400°F/Gas Mark 6, for 20–25 minutes, until the chicken juices run clear when pierced with a skewer.

4 Mix the remaining parsley with the butter and spread evenly over the French bread.

5 Uncover the casserole, arrange the bread slices overlapping on top and bake for a further 10–12 minutes, until golden and crisp.

COOK'S TIP

Add a crushed garlic clove to the parsley butter for extra flavour.

Quick Chicken Dishes

One of the marvellous qualities of chicken is that when cut into small pieces, it can be cooked very quickly, which is welcome for those of us who are too busy to spend a lot of time preparing meals. In this section, you can select a tasty nutritious dish that won't take hours to make. Pasta makes a perfect partner for chicken as it is also quick to cook. Look for Pasta Medley and Italian

Chicken Spirals. Smaller cuts of chicken are also ideal for stir-fries that can be quickly cooked to produce tender, moist and

flavourful chicken. Speedy Peanut Pan-fry is a crunchy stir-fry that is served with noodles, while Chicken & Almond Rissoles with Stir-fried Vegetables offers chicken and potato rissoles with a nutty coating that are served with a colourful mixture of crunchy flash-cooked vegetables.

Chicken with Lemon & Tarragon

Chicken fillets are cooked with saffron, white wine and stock flavoured
with lemon rind and tarragon, then the sauce is thickened with
egg yolks and soured cream and finished with mayonnaise.

Serves 6
6 large skinless, boneless chicken breasts
$1/4$ tsp saffron strands
250 ml/8 fl oz boiling water
1 tbsp olive oil
30 g/1 oz butter
1 garlic clove, crushed
120 ml/4 fl oz dry white wine
grated rind of 1 small lemon
1 tbsp lemon juice
1–2 tbsp chopped fresh tarragon
2 tsp cornflour
1 egg yolk
6 tbsp soured cream
or double cream
4 tbsp thick mayonnaise
salt and pepper

TO GARNISH

sprigs of fresh tarragon
lemon twists

1 Cut each chicken breast almost horizontally into three thin slices with a sharp knife. Season each piece well with salt and pepper.

2 Put the saffron strands into a bowl, pour on the boiling water and leave to stand until needed.

3 Heat the oil, butter and garlic in a frying pan. When foaming, add the chicken and fry on each side until lightly coloured.

4 Add the saffron liquid, wine, lemon rind and juice, and half the tarragon. Bring to the boil, then simmer for about 5 minutes until tender.

5 Remove the chicken with a perforated spoon and place on a serving dish in overlapping slices. Leave to cool. Boil the remaining juices in the pan for 3–4 minutes to reduce slightly.

6 Blend the cornflour, egg yolk and cream together in a bowl. Whisk in a little of the cooking juices, then return to the pan and heat gently, stirring continuously until thickened and just barely simmering. Remove from the heat, adjust the seasoning and pour into a bowl. Cover and leave until cool.

7 Beat the mayonnaise and remaining fresh tarragon into the sauce and spoon over the chicken. Cover and chill thoroughly. Garnish with sprigs of fresh tarragon and lemon twists.

Pasta Medley

Strips of cooked chicken are tossed with coloured pasta, grapes and carrot sticks in a pesto-flavoured dressing. Any leftovers can be kept in the refrigerator for a day or two.

Serves 2

125–150 g/4–5 oz dried pasta shapes, such as twists or bows
1 tbsp oil
2 tbsp mayonnaise
2 tsp bottled pesto sauce
1 tbsp soured cream or natural fromage frais
175 g/6 oz cooked skinless, boneless chicken meat
1–2 celery sticks
125 g/4 oz black grapes (preferably seedless)
1 large carrot, trimmed
salt and pepper
celery leaves, to garnish

FRENCH DRESSING

1 tbsp wine vinegar
3 tbsp extra-virgin olive oil
salt and pepper

1 To make the French dressing, whisk all the ingredients together until smooth.

2 Cook the pasta with the oil for about 12 minutes in plenty of boiling, salted water until just tender. Drain thoroughly, rinse and drain again. Transfer to a bowl and mix in 1 tablespoon of the French dressing while hot; leave until cold.

3 Combine the mayonnaise, pesto sauce and soured cream or fromage frais in a bowl, and season to taste.

4 Cut the chicken into narrow strips. Cut the celery diagonally into narrow

slices. Reserve a few grapes for garnish, halve the rest and remove any pips. Cut the carrot into narrow julienne strips.

5 Add the chicken, the celery, the halved grapes, the carrot and the mayonnaise mixture to the pasta, and

toss thoroughly. Check the seasoning, adding more salt and pepper if necessary.

6 Arrange the pasta medley on two plates and garnish with the reserved black grapes and the celery leaves.

Tagliatelle with Chicken & Almonds

Spinach tagliatelle with a rich tomato sauce and creamy
chicken makes a very appetizing dish.

Serves 4
60 g/2 oz unsalted butter
425 g/14 oz skinless, boneless chicken breasts, sliced thinly
90 g/3 oz blanched almonds
300 ml/$\frac{1}{2}$ pint double cream
250 g/8 oz fresh green ribbon noodles
salt and pepper
basil leaves, to garnish

TOMATO SAUCE

1 small onion, chopped
2 tbsp olive oil
1 garlic clove, chopped
425 g/14 oz can of chopped tomatoes
2 tbsp chopped fresh parsley
1 tsp dried oregano
2 bay leaves
2 tbsp tomato purée
1 tsp sugar

1 To make the tomato sauce, fry the onion gently in the oil until translucent. Add the garlic and fry for 1 minute further. Stir in the remaining ingredients and bring to the boil. Simmer, uncovered, for 15–20 minutes until reduced by half. Discard the bay leaves and keep the sauce warm.

2 Melt the butter and fry the chicken and almonds gently in a pan for 5–6 minutes, stirring frequently.

3 Meanwhile, boil the cream in a small pan for about 10 minutes, until reduced by almost half.

4 Stir the cream into the chicken mixture and season with salt and pepper. Set aside and keep warm.

5 Cook the pasta in a large pan of boiling salted water until just tender.

Drain the pasta and turn into a warmed serving dish.

6 Spoon the tomato sauce over the pasta with the chicken mixture in the centre. Garnish with basil and serve.

Chicken Kiev

This classic dish from the Ukraine is delicious
served with sautéed potatoes.

Serves 4
1 garlic clove, crushed
90 g/3 oz butter
4 skinless, boneless chicken breasts
oil for deep-frying
125 g/4 oz plain flour
2 eggs, beaten
2 tbsp milk
breadcrumbs, for coating
salt and pepper

TO GARNISH

chopped parsley

lemon wedges

1 Mash the garlic into the butter with a fork. Season well and shape into a square patty. Put into the freezer while you prepare the chicken.

2 Slice each chicken breast horizontally in half, and lay between sheets of clingfilm. Flatten each piece to even thickness. Discard the clingfilm.

3 When the butter is quite hard, cut it into four batons. Place a baton lengthways on four of the chicken breast slices. Cover each with another breast slice and refrigerate until ready to serve.

4 Beat the eggs and milk together. When ready to serve, add oil to a pan to a depth of about 5 cm/2 inches and heat to a moderate, deep-frying temperature, 190°C/375°F. Coat each Kiev with flour, then the egg mixture, and finally with breadcrumbs. Repeat once to form a good seal. Fry each Kiev for about 5 minutes. Serve at once while still piping hot.

COOK'S TIP

About 1 tablespoon chopped fresh parsley can be added to the garlic and butter.

Chicken & Almond Rissoles with Stir-fried Vegetables

Cooked potatoes and cooked chicken are combined to make tasty rissoles
rolled in chopped almonds then served with stir-fried vegetables.

Serves 1

125 g/4 oz boiled potatoes
90 g/3 oz carrots
125 g/4 oz cooked chicken meat
1 garlic clove, crushed
1/2 tsp dried tarragon or thyme
generous pinch of ground allspice or ground coriander seeds
1 egg yolk, or 1/2 egg, beaten
about 30 g/1 oz flaked almonds
salt and pepper

STIR-FRIED VEGETABLES

1 celery stick
2 spring onions, trimmed
1 tbsp oil
8 baby sweetcorn cobs
about 10–12 mangetout or sugar snap peas, trimmed
2 tsp balsamic vinegar
salt and pepper

1 Grate the boiled potatoes and raw carrots coarsely into a bowl. Chop finely or mince the chicken and add to the vegetables with the garlic, tarragon, allspice or coriander and plenty of salt and pepper.

2 Add the egg yolk or beaten egg and bind the ingredients together. Divide in half and shape into sausages.

3 Chop the almonds evenly and then roll each rissole in the nuts until evenly coated.

4 Place the rissoles in a greased ovenproof dish and cook in a preheated oven, 200°C/400°F/Gas Mark 6, for about 20 minutes or until lightly browned; alternatively, fry in a little oil until browned all over and cooked through.

5 While the rissoles cook, prepare the stir-fried vegetables. Cut the celery and spring onions on the diagonal into narrow slices. Heat the oil in a frying pan and toss in the vegetables. Cook over a high heat for 1–2 minutes, then add the sweetcorn cobs and peas, and cook for 2–3 minutes. Finally, add the balsamic vinegar and season with salt and pepper to taste.

6 Spoon the stir-fried vegetables on to a serving plate and place the rissoles beside them. Serve at once.

Chicken with Peanut Sauce

A tangy stir-fry with a strong peanut flavour.
Serve with freshly boiled rice or noodles.

Serves 4
4 skinless, boneless chicken breasts, weighing 625 g/1¼ lb
4 tbsp soy sauce
4 tbsp sherry
3 tbsp crunchy peanut butter
350 g/12 oz courgettes, trimmed
2 tbsp sunflower oil
4–6 spring onions, thinly sliced diagonally
250 g/8 oz can of bamboo shoots, well drained and sliced
salt and pepper
4 tbsp desiccated coconut, toasted, to garnish

1 Cut the chicken into thin strips across the grain and season lightly with salt and pepper.

2 Put the soy sauce in a bowl with the sherry and peanut butter, and stir until smooth and well blended.

3 Cut the courgettes into 5 cm/2 inch lengths and then cut into sticks about 5 mm/¼ inch thick.

4 Heat the oil in the wok, swirling it around until it is really hot. Add the spring onions and stir-fry for a minute or so, then add the chicken and stir-fry for 3–4 minutes until well sealed and almost cooked.

5 Add the courgettes and bamboo shoots and continue to stir-fry for 1–2 minutes.

6 Add the peanut butter mixture and heat thoroughly, stirring all the time so everything is coated in the sauce as it thickens. Adjust the seasoning and serve very hot, sprinkled with the toasted coconut.

COOK'S TIP

If you prefer, smooth peanut butter can be used instead of the crunchy variety.

Chicken with Celery & Cashew Nuts

Yellow bean sauce, widely available bottled, gives this easy Chinese dish a really
authentic taste. Pecan nuts can be used in place of the cashews.

Serves 4

3–4 skinless, boneless chicken
breasts, weighing 625g/1¼ lb

2 tbsp sunflower
or vegetable oil

125 g/4 oz unsalted
cashew nuts

4–6 spring onions,
sliced thinly diagonally

5–6 celery sticks, thinly
sliced diagonally

175 g/6 oz jar of stir-fry
yellow bean sauce

salt and pepper

celery leaves, to garnish
(optional)

boiled rice, to serve

1 Cut the chicken into thin slices across the grain.

2 Heat the oil in the wok, swirling it around until really hot. Add the cashew nuts and stir-fry until they begin to brown, then add the chicken and stir-fry until well sealed and almost cooked through.

3 Add the spring onions and celery and continue to stir-fry for 2–3 minutes, stirring the ingredients well around the wok.

4 Add the yellow bean sauce, season lightly with salt and pepper and toss until the chicken and vegetables are thoroughly coated with the sauce and piping hot. Serve at once with plain boiled rice, garnished with celery leaves, if liked.

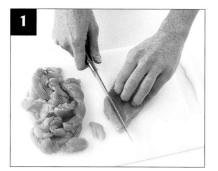

Pan-cooked Chicken with Artichokes

Artichokes are a familiar ingredient in Italian cookery.
In this dish, they are used as a delicate flavouring with chicken.

Serves 4
4 chicken breasts, part boned
2 tbsp olive oil
30 g/1 oz butter
2 red onions, cut into wedges
2 tbsp lemon juice
150 ml/¼ pt dry white wine
150 ml/¼ pt chicken stock
2 tsp plain flour
425 g/14 oz can of artichoke hearts, drained and halved
salt and pepper
chopped fresh parsley, to garnish

1 Season the chicken with salt and freshly ground black pepper. Heat the oil and 15 g/½ oz of the butter in a large frying pan. Add the chicken and fry gently for 4–5 minutes on each side until lightly golden. Remove from the pan using a perforated spoon.

2 Toss the onions in the lemon juice, and add to the frying pan. Fry gently, stirring, for 3–4 minutes until just beginning to soften.

3 Return the chicken to the pan. Pour in the wine and stock, bring to the boil, then cover and simmer gently for 30 minutes.

4 Remove the chicken from the pan, reserving the cooking juices. Keep warm. Bring the juices to the boil, and boil rapidly for 5 minutes.

5 Blend the remaining butter with the flour to form a paste. Reduce the pan juices to a simmer and add the paste to the frying pan, stirring until thickened.

6 Adjust the seasoning, stir in the artichokes and cook for a further 2 minutes. Pour over the chicken and garnish with parsley.

Poached Breast of Chicken with Whisky Sauce

After cooking with stock and vegetables, chicken breasts are served with a velvety sauce made from whisky and crème fraîche.

Serves 4
30 g/1 oz butter
60 g/2 oz shredded leeks
60 g/2 oz diced carrot
60 g/2 oz diced celery
4 shallots, sliced
600 ml/1 pint chicken stock
6 chicken breasts
50 ml/2 fl oz whisky
200 ml/7 fl oz crème fraîche
2 tbsp freshly grated horseradish
1 tsp honey, warmed
1 tsp chopped fresh parsley
salt and pepper
parsley, to garnish

1 Melt the butter in a large saucepan and add the leeks, carrot, celery and shallots. Cook for 3 minutes, add half the chicken stock and cook for about 8 minutes.

2 Add the remaining chicken stock, bring to the boil, add the chicken breasts and cook for 10 minutes.

3 Remove the chicken and thinly slice. Place on a large, hot serving dish and keep warm.

4 In another saucepan, heat the whisky until reduced by half. Strain the chicken stock through a fine sieve, add to the pan and reduce the liquid by half.

5 Add the crème fraîche, the horseradish and the honey. Heat gently and add the parsley and salt and pepper to taste.

6 Pour a little of the whisky sauce around the chicken and pour the remaining sauce into a sauceboat to serve.

7 Serve with a vegetable patty made from the leftover vegetables, mashed potato and fresh vegetables. Garnish with parsley.

Garlicky Chicken Cushions

Stuffed with creamy ricotta, spinach and garlic, then gently cooked in
a rich tomato sauce, this is a suitable dish to make ahead of time.

Serves 4
4 part-boned chicken breasts
125 g/4 oz frozen spinach, defrosted
150 g/5 oz ricotta cheese
2 garlic cloves, crushed
1 tbsp olive oil
1 onion, chopped
1 red pepper, sliced
425 g/14 oz can chopped tomatoes
6 tbsp wine or chicken stock
10 stuffed olives, sliced
salt and pepper
flat leaf parsley sprigs, to garnish

1 Make a slit between the skin and meat on one side of each chicken breast. Lift the skin to form a pocket, being careful to leave the skin attached to the other side.

2 Put the spinach into a sieve and press out the water with a spoon. Mix with the ricotta, half the garlic and seasoning.

3 Spoon the spinach mixture under the skin of each chicken breast then secure the edge of the skin with cocktail sticks.

4 Heat the oil in a frying pan, add the onion and fry for a minute, stirring. Add the remaining garlic and red (bell) pepper and cook for 2 minutes. Stir in the tomatoes, wine or stock, olives and seasoning. Set the sauce aside and chill the chicken if preparing in advance.

5 Bring the sauce to the boil, pour into a shallow ovenproof dish and arrange the chicken breasts on top in a single layer.

6 Cook, uncovered in a preheated oven, 200°C/400°F/Gas Mark 6, for 35 minutes until the chicken is golden and cooked through. Test by making a slit in one of the chicken breasts with a skewer to make sure the juices run clear. Spoon a little of the sauce over the chicken breasts then transfer to serving plates and garnish with parsley. Serve with pasta.

Mediterranean Chicken Parcels

This method of cooking makes the chicken aromatic and succulent.

Serves 6
1 tbsp olive oil
6 skinless chicken breast fillets
250 g/8 oz mozzarella cheese
500 g/1 lb courgettes, sliced
6 large tomatoes, sliced
1 small bunch fresh basil or oregano
pepper

1 Cut six pieces of foil each about 25cm/10in square. Brush the foil squares lightly with oil.

2 With a sharp knife, slash each chicken breast at intervals, then slice the cheese and place between the cuts in the chicken.

3 Divide the courgettes and tomatoes between the pieces of foil and sprinkle with black pepper. Tear or roughly chop the herbs and scatter over the vegetables.

4 Place the chicken on top of each pile of vegetables then wrap in the foil to enclose the chicken and vegetables, tucking in the ends.

5 Place on a baking sheet and bake in a preheated oven, 200°C/400°C/Gas Mark 6, for about 30 minutes. To serve, unwrap each foil parcel and serve with rice or pasta.

Steamed Chicken & Spring Vegetable Parcels

A healthy recipe with a delicate oriental flavour, ideal for tender young summer vegetables. You'll need large spinach leaves to wrap around the chicken, but make sure they are young leaves.

Serves 4
4 boneless, skinless British chicken breasts
1 tsp ground lemon grass
2 spring onions, chopped finely
250 g/8 oz young carrots
250 g/8 oz young courgettes
2 sticks celery
1 tsp light soy sauce
250 g/8 oz spinach leaves
2 tsp sesame oil
salt and pepper

1 With a sharp knife, make a slit through one side of each chicken breast, to open out a large pocket. Sprinkle the inside of the pocket with lemon grass, salt and pepper. Tuck the spring onions into the chicken pockets.

2 Trim the carrots, courgettes and celery then cut into small matchsticks. Plunge them into a pan of boiling water for 1 minute, then drain and toss in the soy sauce.

3 Pack into the pockets in each chicken breast and fold over firmly to enclose. Reserve the remaining vegetables. Wash and dry the spinach leaves then wrap the chicken breasts firmly in the leaves to enclose completely. If the leaves are too firm to wrap the chicken easily, steam them for a few seconds until they are softened and flexible.

4 Place the wrapped chicken in a steamer and steam over rapidly boiling water for 20–25 minutes, depending on size.

5 Stir-fry any leftover vegetable sticks and spinach for 1–2 minutes in the sesame oil and serve with the chicken.

Parma Wrapped Chicken Cushions

Stuffed with creamy ricotta, nutmeg and spinach, then wrapped with wafer thin
slices of Parma ham and gently cooked in white wine.

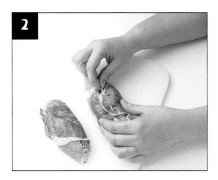

Serves 4
125 g/4 oz frozen spinach, defrosted
125 g/4 oz ricotta cheese
pinch grated nutmeg
4 skinless, boneless chicken breasts, each weighing 175 g/6 oz
4 Parma ham slices
30 g/1 oz butter
1 tbsp olive oil
12 small onions or shallots
125 g/4 oz button mushrooms, sliced
1 tbsp plain flour
150 ml/¼ pint dry white or red wine
300 ml/½ pint chicken stock
flat leaf parsley sprigs, to garnish

1 Put the spinach into a sieve and press out the water with a spoon. Mix with the ricotta and nutmeg and season with salt and pepper.

2 Slit each chicken breast through the side and enlarge each cut to form a pocket. Fill with the spinach mixture, reshape the chicken breasts, wrap each in a slice of ham and secure with cocktail sticks. Cover and chill.

3 Heat the butter and oil in a frying pan and brown the chicken breasts for 2 minutes on each side. Transfer the chicken to a large, shallow ovenproof dish.

4 Fry the onions and mushrooms for 2–3 minutes until lightly browned.

Stir in the flour then gradually add the wine and stock. Bring to the boil, stirring. Season and spoon the mixture around the chicken.

5 Cook the chicken uncovered in a preheated oven, 200°C/400°F/Gas Mark 6, for 20 minutes. Turn the breasts over and cook for a further 10 minutes. Remove the cocktail sticks and serve with the sauce. Garnish with the parsley and serve with carrot purée and green beans, if wished.

Chicken Lady Jayne

If you prefer just use boneless chicken breasts in this recipe.
This dish has a surprising combination of coffee and brandy flavours.

Serves 4
500 g/1 lb chicken breasts or supremes
4 tbsp corn oil
8 shallots, sliced
rind and juice of 1 lemon
2 tsp Worcestershire sauce
4 tbsp chicken stock
1 tbsp chopped fresh parsley
3 tbsp coffee liqueur
3 tbsp brandy, warmed

1 Cut the chicken breasts into 4 even pieces, cover them with cling film and beat them flat with a wooden meat mallet or a rolling pin.

2 Heat the oil in a large frying pan and fry the chicken for 3 minutes on each side, add the shallots and cook for a further 3 minutes.

3 Sprinkle with lemon juice and lemon rind and add the Worcestershire sauce and chicken stock. Cook for 2 minutes, then sprinkle with the parsley. Finally, add the coffee liqueur and the brandy and flame the chicken by lighting the spirit with a taper or long match. Cook until the flame is extinguished and serve.

COOK'S TIP

A supreme is a chicken fillet that sometimes has part of the wing bone remaining. Chicken breasts can be used instead.

Savoury Chicken Sausages

Served with a smooth creamy tomato sauce,
this makes an excellent light lunch with freshly baked cheese bread.

Serves 4–6
175 g/6 oz fresh breadcrumbs
250 g/8 oz cooked chicken, minced
1 small leek, chopped finely
pinch each of mixed herbs and mustard powder
2 eggs, separated
4 tbsp milk
crisp breadcrumbs for coating
30 g/1 of beef dripping
salt and pepper

1 In a large clean bowl, mix together the breadcrumbs, chicken, leek, herbs and mustard powder, and season with salt and pepper.

2 Add 1 whole egg and an egg yollk with a little milk to bind the mixture.

3 Divide the mixture into 6 or 8 and shape into thick or thin sausages.

4 Whisk the remaining egg white until frothy. Coat the sausages first in the egg white and then in the crisp breadcrumbs.

5 Heat the dripping and fry the sausages for 6 minutes until golden brown. Serve the sausages with a little tomato sauce.

COOK'S VARIATION

If you want to lower saturated fat in this recipe, use a little oil for frying instead of the dripping.

Tom's Toad in the Hole

This unusual recipe uses chicken and Cumberland sausage,
which is then made into individual bite-sized cakes.

Serves 4–6
125 g/4 oz plain flour
pinch of salt
1 egg, beaten
200 ml/7 fl oz milk
75 ml/3 fl oz water
250 g/8 oz chicken breasts
250 g/ 8 oz Cumberland sausage
2 tbsp beef dripping

1 Mix the flour and salt in a bowl, make a well in the centre and add the beaten egg.

2 Add half the milk, and using a wooden spoon, work in the flour slowly.

3 Beat the mixture until it is smooth, then add the remaining milk and water.

4 Beat again until the mixture is smooth. Let the mixture stand for at least 1 hour. Add the dripping to individual baking tins or to one large baking tin.

5 Cut up the chicken and sausage so that you get a generous piece in each individual tin or several scattered around the large tin.

6 Heat the tins in a preheated oven, 220°C/425°F/Gas Mark 7, for 5 minutes until very hot. Remove the tins from the oven and pour in the batter, leaving space for the mixture to expand.

7 Return to the oven to cook for 35 minutes, until risen and golden brown. Do not open the oven door for at least 30 minutes.

8 Serve while hot, with chicken or onion gravy, or alone.

COOK'S VARIATION

Use skinless, boneless chicken legs instead of chicken breast in the recipe. Cut up as directed. Instead of Cumberland sausage, use your favourite variety of sausage.

Devilled Chicken

Chicken is spiked with cayenne and paprika and finished off with a fruity sauce.

Serves 2–3
30 g/1 oz plain flour
1 tbsp cayenne pepper
1 tsp paprika
350 g/12 oz skinless, boneless chicken, diced
30 g/1 oz butter
1 onion, chopped finely
450 ml/$^3/_4$ pint milk, warmed
4 tbsp apple purée
125 g/4 oz/$^3/_4$ cup green grapes
150 ml/$^1/_4$ pint soured cream.
sprinkle of paprika

1 Mix the flour, cayenne and paprika together and use to coat the chicken.

2 Shake off any excess flour. Melt the butter in a saucepan and gently fry the chicken with the onion for 4 minutes.

3 Stir in the flour and spice mixture and slowly blend in the milk, stirring until the sauce thickens.

4 Simmer until the sauce is smooth.

5 Add the apple purée and grapes and simmer gently for 20 minutes.

6 Transfer the chicken and devilled sauce to a serving dish and top with soured cream and a sprinkle of paprika.

Quick Chicken Bake

This recipe is a type of cottage pie and is just as versatile. Add vegetables and herbs of your choice, depending on what you have at hand.

Serves 4
500 g/1 lb minced chicken
1 large onion, chopped finely
2 carrots, diced finely
30 g/1 oz/2 tbsp plain flour
1 tbsp tomato purée
300 ml/1¹/₂ pint chicken stock
pinch of fresh thyme
900 g/1³/₄ lb potatoes, creamed with butter and milk and highly seasoned
90 g/3 oz grated Lancashire cheese
salt and pepper

1 Dry-fry the minced chicken, onion and carrots in a non-stick saucepan for 5 minutes.

2 Sprinkle the chicken with the flour and simmer for a further 2 minutes.

3 Gradually blend in the tomato purée and stock then simmer for 15 minutes. Season and add the thyme.

4 Transfer the chicken mixture to an oven proof casserole and allow to cool.

5 Top the chicken with the mashed potato and sprinkle with the cheese. Bake in a preheated oven, 200°C/400°F/Gas Mark 6, for 20 minutes, then serve with peas.

Chicken in Rum & Orange Cream Sauce

A rich, orange cream sauce that is simplicity itself. Its luxurious texture comes from crème fraîche, but you can use single cream instead.

Serves 4
2 tbsp sunflower oil
8 small, skinless chicken drumsticks
3 shallots or spring onions, chopped finely
200 ml/7 floz orange juice
4 tbsp dark rum
250 g/8 oz long grain rice
grated rind of $1/2$ orange
200 ml/7 floz crème fraîche or single cream
salt and pepper
orange segments (optional) and parsley to garnish

1 Heat the oil in a large pan and fry the chicken and the onions over a moderate heat until browned.

2 Add the orange juice and rum, cover tightly and simmer for 15 minutes or until the chicken juices run clear, not pink, when pierced with a skewer.

3 Meanwhile, cook the rice in boiling, lightly salted water until just tender. Drain and stir in the orange rind.

4 Stir the crème fraîche into the chicken and bring to the boil.

5 Season. Serve the chicken with the orange rice, garnished with orange segments, if using, and parsley.

Speedy Peanut Pan-fry

A complete main course cooked within ten minutes. Thread egg noodles are the ideal accompaniment because they can be cooked quickly and easily while the stir-fry sizzles, but any type of pasta or rice can be served instead.

Serves 4
300 g/10 oz courgettes
250 g/8 oz baby corn
250 g/8 oz thread egg noodles
2 tbsp corn oil
1 tbsp sesame oil
8 boneless chicken thighs or 4 breasts, sliced thinly
300 g/10 oz button mushrooms
350 g/12 oz beansprouts
4 tbsp smooth peanut butter
2 tbsp soy sauce
2 tbsp lime or lemon juice
60 g/2 oz roasted peanuts
salt and pepper
coriander, to garnish

1 Trim and thinly slice the courgettes and corn.

2 Cook the noodles in lightly salted boiling water for 3–4 minutes Meanwhile, heat the oils in a large frying pan or wok and fry the chicken over a fairly high heat for 1 minute.

3 Add the courgettes, corn and mushrooms and stir-fry for 5 minutes.

4 Add the beansprouts, peanut butter, soy sauce, lime juice and pepper, then cook for a further 2 minutes.

5 Drain the noodles. Scatter with the peanuts and serve with the noodles. Garnish with coriander.

Italian Chicken Spirals

Steaming allows you to cook without fat, and these little foil parcels retain all the natural juices
of the chicken while cooking conveniently over the pasta while it boils. Sun-dried tomatoes, preserved in oil, have a
wonderful, rich flavour, but if you can't find them use fresh tomatoes.

Serves 4
4 skinless, boneless, chicken breasts
30 g/1 oz fresh basil leaves
15 g/^{1}/$_2$ oz hazelnuts
1 garlic clove, crushed
250 g/8 oz wholemeal pasta spirals
2 sun-dried tomatoes or fresh tomatoes
1 tbsp lemon juice
1 tbsp olive oil
1 tbsp capers
60 g/2 oz black olives
salt and pepper
sprigs of basil, to garnish

1 Beat the chicken breasts with a rolling pin to flatten evenly.

2 Place the basil and hazelnuts in a food processor and process until finely chopped. Mix with the garlic, salt and pepper.

3 Spread the basil mixture over the chicken breasts and roll up from one short end to enclose the filling. Wrap the chicken roll tightly in foil so that they hold their shape, then seal the ends well.

4 Add the pasta to a large pan of lightly salted, boiling water. Place the chicken parcels in a steamer basket or colander set over the pan, cover tightly, and steam for 10 minutes. Meanwhile, dice the tomatoes.

5 Drain the pasta and return to the pan with the lemon juice, olive oil,

tomatoes, capers and olives. Heat until warmed through.

6 Pierce the chicken with a skewer to make sure that the juices run clear

and not pink, then slice the chicken and arrange over the pasta. Garnish with sprigs of basil and serve with a tomato salad.

Harlequin Chicken

This colourful, simple dish will tempt the appetites of all the family – it is ideal for toddlers, who enjoy the fun shapes of the multi-coloured peppers.

Serves 4
10 skinless, boneless chicken thighs
1 medium onion
1 each medium red, green and yellow peppers
1 tbsp sunflower oil
425 g/14oz can chopped tomatoes
2 tbsp chopped fresh parsley
pepper

1 Cut the chicken thighs into bite-sized pieces.

2 Peel and thinly slice the onion. Halve and deseed the peppers and cut into small diamond shapes.

3 Heat the oil in a shallow pan then quickly fry the chicken and onion until golden.

4 Add the peppers, cook for 2–3 minutes, then stir in the tomatoes and parsley and season with pepper.

5 Cover tightly and simmer for about 15 minutes, until the chicken and vegetables are tender. Serve hot with wholemeal bread and a green salad.

COOK'S TIP

If you are making this dish for small children, the chicken can be finely chopped or minced first.

Golden Chicken Risotto

If you prefer, ordinary long grain rice can be used instead of risotto rice, but it won't give you the traditional, deliciously creamy texture that is typical of Italian risottos.

Serves 4
2tbsp sunflower oil
15 g/½ oz butter or margarine
1 medium leek, thinly sliced
1 large yellow pepper, diced
3 skinless, boneless chicken breasts, diced
350 g/12 oz round grain rice
few strands saffron
1.5 litres/2½ pints chicken stock
200 g/7 oz can sweetcorn
60 g/2 oz toasted unsalted peanuts
60 g/2 oz grated Parmesan cheese
salt and pepper

1 In a large pan, heat the oil and butter. Fry the leek and pepper for 1 minute then stir in the chicken and cook, stirring until golden brown.

2 Stir in the rice and cook for 2–3 minutes.

3 Add the saffron, stock, salt and pepper. Cover and cook over a low heat, stirring occasionally, for about 20 minutes, until the rice is tender and most of the liquid is absorbed. Add more stock if necessary.

4 Stir in the sweetcorn, peanuts and Parmesan cheese, then adjust the seasoning to taste.

5 Serve hot with a crisp green salad.

Elizabethan Chicken

Chicken is surprisingly delicious when combined
with fruits such as grapes or gooseberries.

Serves 4
15 g/$^1/_2$ oz butter
1 tbsp sunflower oil
4 skinless. boneless chicken breasts
4 shallots, finely chopped
150 ml/$^1/_2$ pint chicken stock
1 tbsp cider vinegar
175 g/ 6 oz halved seedless grapes
120 ml/4 floz double cream
1 tsp freshly grated nutmeg
cornflour, to thicken, (optional)
salt and pepper

1 Heat the butter and oil in a wide. flameproof casserole or pan and quickly fry the chicken breasts until golden brown, turning once. Remove and keep hot.

2 Add the shallots to the pan and fry gently until softened and lightly browned. Return the chicken breasts to the pan.

3 Add the stock and vinegar, bring to the boil then cover and simmer gently for 10–12 minutes, stirring.

4 Transfer the chicken to a serving dish. Add the grapes, cream and nutmeg. Heat through, season to taste and serve hot. Thicken with a little cornflour if desired.

Chicken, Corn & Mangetout Sauté

This quick and healthy dish is stir-fried, which means you need use only the minimum of fat. If you don't have a wok, use a wide frying pan instead.

Serves 4
4 skinless, boneless chicken breasts
250 g/8 oz baby sweetcorn
250 g/8 oz mangetout
2 tbsp sunflower oil
1 tbsp sherry vinegar
1 tbsp honey
1 tbsp light soy sauce
1 tbsp sunflower seeds
pepper

1 Slice the chicken breasts into long, thin strips. Cut the corn cobs in half lengthways and top and tail the mangetout.

2 Heat the oil in a wok or a wide frying pan and fry the chicken over a fairly high heat, stirring, for 1 minute.

3 Add the corn and mangetout and stir over a moderate heat for 5–8 minutes, until evenly cooked.

4 Mix together the sherry vinegar, honey and soy sauce and stir into the pan with the sunflower seeds. Season well with pepper. Cook, stirring, for 1 minute. Serve hot with rice or Chinese egg noodles.

COOK'S TIP

Rice vinegar or balsamic vinegar makes a good substitute for the sherry vinegar.

Chicken with Two Pepper Sauce

This quick and simple dish is colourful and healthy. It would be perfect for
an impromptu lunch or supper dish.

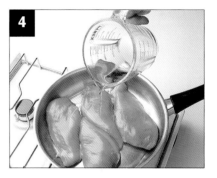

Serves 4
2 tbsp olive oil
2 medium onions, chopped finely
2 garlic cloves, crushed
2 red peppers, chopped
good pinch cayenne pepper
2 tsp tomato purée
2 yellow peppers, chopped
pinch of dried basil
4 skinless, boneless chicken breasts
150 ml/¼ pint dry white wine
150 ml/¼ pint chicken stock
bouquet garni
salt and pepper
fresh herbs, to garnish

1 Heat 1 tablespoon of oil in each of two medium saucepans. Place half the chopped onions, 1 of the garlic cloves, the red peppers, the cayenne pepper and the tomato purée in one of the saucepans. Place the remaining onion, garlic, yellow peppers and basil in the other pan.

2 Cover each pan and cook over a very low heat for 1 hour until the peppers are very soft. If either mixture becomes dry, add a little water. Process then sieve the contents of each pan separately.

3 Return to the pans and season with salt and pepper. The two sauces can be gently re-heated while the chicken is cooking.

4 Put the chicken breasts into a frying pan and add the wine and stock. Add the bouquet garni and bring the liquid to simmer. Cook the chicken for about 20 minutes until tender.

5 To serve, put a pool of each sauce onto four serving plates, slice the chicken breasts and arrange on the plates. Garnish with fresh herbs.

Pies, Pastries & Terrines

Chicken once again shows its versatility in a splendid array of pastries and pies. Many of the pies and terrines can be made ahead of time and served cold, making them a good choice for a buffet, picnic or packed lunch. A thin slice of a terrine or pie can be served as a starter or a light meal, while a hearty slice of a traditional pie, such as Raised Chicken Pie, served with pickles and

salad, makes a satisfying main course. Various pastries are used for the pies, a choux pastry topping adorns

Chicken and Sweetcorn Puff, while Sesame Chicken Pies, Chicken Filo Parcels and Stilton & Walnut Strudel are all made from sheets of filo pastry. A suet pastry is used to make Old Fashioned Chicken Pudding and for Chicken, Cheese & Tarragon Pie, the base is made from shortcrust pastry while the topping is a golden puff pastry.

Chicken & Sweetcorn Puff

This delicious choux puff is an impressive dish yet it's simple to make.
You can use the choux pastry as a topping for all kinds of filling.

Serves 4
30 g/1 oz butter
or margarine
30 g/1 oz plain flour
300 ml/$\frac{1}{2}$ pint
skimmed milk
250 g/8 oz skinless, boneless
cooked chicken, shredded
125 g/4 oz can sweetcorn, drained
1 tbsp chopped fresh parsley
salt and pepper

CHOUX PASTRY

75 g/2$\frac{1}{2}$ oz plain flour
60 g/2 oz butter or margarine
150 ml water
2 eggs, beaten
salt

5 Spoon the choux pastry around the edge of the dish. Bake in a preheated oven, 220°C/425°F/Gas Mark 7, for 35–40 minutes until puffed up and golden brown. Serve at once.

1 To make the choux pastry, sift the flour and salt into a bowl. Put the butter or margarine and water into a pan, then heat gently until the butter has melted. Bring to the boil. Remove from the heat and add the flour all at once. Beat with a wooden spoon until the mixture leaves the sides of the pan clean. Leave to cool slightly.

2 Gradually beat in the eggs until the mixture is thick and very glossy.

3 To make the filling, put the butter or margarine, flour and milk into a saucepan. Heat, whisking constantly, until smooth and thickened.

4 Add the chicken, sweetcorn and parsley, and season to taste. Pour into a 1 litre/1¾ pint shallow baking dish.

Three Fillet Parcel

Fillets of chicken, lamb and pork are layered with sage leaves, wrapped in spinach
leaves, covered with a layer of cottage cheese and enclosed in puff pastry.
This is delicious served cold and cut into slices.

Serves 6

300–350 g/10–12 oz pork fillet
or tenderloin

about 12 fresh sage leaves

250–300 g/8–10 oz lamb neck fillet

2 skinless, boneless chicken breast fillets,
weighing 300 g/10 oz

2 tbsp oil

125 g/4 oz large spinach leaves

350 g/12 oz puff pastry,
thawed if frozen

250 g/8 oz cottage cheese

pinch of ground allspice

pinch of garlic powder

beaten egg or milk to glaze

salt and pepper

TO GARNISH

sage leaves

cucumber slices

1 Layer the fillets beginning with the pork fillet. Cover with half the sage leaves, then add the lamb fillet, the rest of the sage leaves and finally the chicken fillets. Secure with string.

2 Heat the oil in a frying pan and fry the layered fillets for about 15 minutes, turning until browned and partly cooked. Remove from the pan and leave until cold.

3 Blanch the spinach leaves in boiling water for 2 minutes and drain well.

4 Roll out the pastry thinly into a rectangle large enough to enclose the layered fillets and allow for five narrow strips to be cut off the edge.

Cut off the strips, then lay the spinach in the centre of the pastry. Spread with the cottage cheese. Season and add the allspice and garlic powder.

5 Remove the string and place the fillets on top of the cheese and spinach. Wrap up in the pastry and seal the edges. Stand on a greased

baking sheet and glaze with egg. Lay strips of pastry over the roll and glaze.

6 Bake in a preheated oven, 200°C/400°F/Gas Mark 6, for 30 minutes. Reduce the temperature to 180°C/350°F/Gas Mark 4 and bake for 20 minutes. Cool, then chill. Slice and garnish with sage and cucumber.

Raised Chicken Pie

A filling of diced chicken leg meat, minced pork and bacon with pickled walnuts, mushrooms and herbs is enclosed in a hot-water pastry crust.

Serves 6
350 g/12 oz skinless, boneless chicken thighs
125 g/4 oz lean raw pork, minced
125 g/4 oz cooked ham, minced coarsely or chopped finely
1 small onion, very finely chopped
60 g/2 oz button mushrooms, chopped roughly
1 tbsp chopped fresh parsley
good pinch of ground coriander seeds
6 pickled walnuts, well drained
beaten egg or milk to glaze
1 tsp powdered gelatine
150 ml/¼ pint chicken stock
salt and pepper

PASTRY

350 g/12 oz plain flour
1 tsp salt
90 g/3 oz lard
6 tbsp water
3 tbsp milk, for glazing

1 To make the filling, chop the chicken thighs and mix with the pork, ham, onion, mushrooms, parsley and ground coriander, and seasoning.

2 To make the pastry, sift the flour and salt into a bowl. Melt the lard in a saucepan with the water and milk and then bring to the boil. Pour onto the flour and mix to an even dough.

3 Roll out about three-quarters of the dough and use to line a lightly greased raised pie mould or a loaf tin.

4 Add half the chicken mixture to the mould, then a layer of walnuts and the remaining chicken. Roll out the reserved pastry, position over the chicken as a lid and cut a hole in the centre. Add pastry leaves and glaze.

5 Bake on a baking sheet in a preheated oven, 200°C/400°F/Gas Mark 6, for 30 minutes. Reduce the temperature to 180°C/350°F/Gas Mark 4, glaze and bake for 1 hour. Remove from the oven. Cool for 10 minutes.

6 Dissolve the gelatine in the stock. Add as much stock as possible through the lid. Cool down then chill for 12 hours. Unmould before serving.

Sussex Huffed Pie

This modern version of a very old English classic uses chicken breasts wrapped in a light and crisp crust of vegetable suet crust pastry. The Bramley and walnut stuffing adds a delicious moist filling to each little parcel.

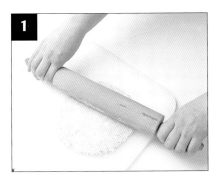

Serves 4
350 g/12 oz self-raising flour, sifted
175 g/6 oz vegetable suet
4 skinless, boneless chicken breasts
1 small Bramley apple, sliced thinly
30 g/1 oz chopped walnuts
2 tbsp chopped fresh sage
2 tbsp Worcester sauce
milk, to glaze
salt and pepper

1 Mix the flour and suet, and season. Stir in just enough cold water to bind to a firm, but not sticky dough. Divide into 4 and roll out each piece of dough to a 20 cm/8 inch round.

2 Cut a slit in the side of each chicken breast and pack with apple slices, walnuts and sage. Brush the pastry rounds all over with Worcester sauce.

3 Place a chicken breast on each pastry round.

4 Fold the pastry over and pinch the edges of the pastry together to seal. Lift onto a baking sheet and glaze with milk. Bake in a preheated oven, 200°C/400°F/Gas Mark 6, for 30–35 minutes until golden brown. Serve hot or cold.

Nell Gwynn's Chicken Pie

A traditional old English type of pie, subtly flavoured with oranges. If you prefer, it can be made with chicken off the bone instead of joints.

Serves 4
8 skinless chicken joints (drumsticks and thighs)
200 g/7 oz baby onions
1 large orange
120 ml/4 floz chicken stock
250 g/8 oz chilled or frozen puff pastry, thawed
milk, for brushing
salt and pepper

FORCEMEAT

90 g/3 oz/1½ cups fresh wholemeal breadcrumbs
30 g/1 oz finely chopped cooked ham
2 tbsp chopped fresh parsley
finely grated rind 1 orange
1 tbsp sunflower oil
1 egg, beaten

1 Mix together all the ingredients for the forcemeat and season well with salt and pepper. Shape the mixture into 8 small balls.

2 Fry the chicken joints in a non-stick pan without fat, turning occasionally until golden brown. Drain and transfer to a 1.7 litre/3 pint pie dish.

3 Plunge the onions into a pan of boiling water and boil for 1 minute. Drain, rinse in cold water and remove the skins.

4 Cut away all the peel and white pith from the orange, then remove the segments. Add the onions, orange and forcemeat balls to the dish. Add the stock and season.

5 Roll out the pastry slightly larger than the pie dish and cut a 2.5 cm/ 1 inch wide strip from the edge. Brush the rim of the dish with milk and press on the strip of pastry to fit.

6 Cover the pie with the large piece of pastry. Press the edges to seal and brush with the milk. Place on a baking sheet in a preheated oven, 220°C/425°F/Gas Mark 7, for 10 minutes. Reduce the heat to 160°C/325°F/Gas Mark 3 and bake for a further hour. Serve hot with fresh green vegetables.

Chicken, Stilton & Walnut Strudel

A perfect choice for a cold buffet table, or serve hot with a red wine gravy for a dinner party main course. The combination of Stilton, mushrooms and walnuts helps enrich and moisten the filling without the need for a sauce to bind the ingredients. The strudel slices more easily when cold.

Serves 5–6
60 g/2 oz butter
175 g/6 oz oyster or flat mushrooms, sliced
2 shallots or spring onions, chopped finely
500 g/1 lb boneless, cooked chicken thighs, chopped finely
60 g/2 oz walnut pieces
150 g/5 oz Stilton cheese, crumbled
3 tbsp fromage frais
1 tbsp chopped fresh thyme
7 sheets of filo pastry, each measuring 7$^1/_2$ x14 inches/19 x 35 cm
pepper

1 Melt 2 tablespoons butter and fry the mushrooms, shallots and chicken until the shallots are softened and any free liquid has evaporated.

2 Reserve a few walnuts for garnish and combine the rest with the mushrooms, shallots, chicken, Stilton cheese, fromage frais and thyme. Season with pepper.

3 Melt the remaining butter. Brush each sheet of pastry with butter then overlap the sheets to make one large square. Spoon the chicken mixture into the centre of the square.

4 Roll up carefully to enclose the filling, tucking in the ends.

5 Lift the roll carefully onto a greased baking sheet, brush with butter and scatter with the remaining walnuts.

Bake in a preheated oven, 190°C/375°F/Gas Mark 5, for 25–30 minutes until golden brown and firm. Serve hot or cold, with salad or vegetables.

COOK'S TIP

Fromage frais is a fresh curd cheese that varies in fat content. It is available both fat-free and with 8 percent fat.

Chicken Filo Parcels

Perfect for a picnic or a packed lunch, these tasty chicken parcels can
be packed into a rigid plastic container for carrying.

Serves 6
150 g/5 oz frozen spinach, thawed
150 g/5 oz feta cheese
6 skinless, boneless chicken thighs
12 sheets filo pastry, each measuring 7$^1/_2$ x14 inches/ 19 x 35 cm
2 tbsp sunflower oil
1 tbsp poppy seeds
pepper

1 Place the spinach in a sieve and press out excess moisture. Crumble the cheese then mix with the spinach and season with pepper.

2 Open out the chicken thighs on a board and place a spoonful of the spinach mixture on each. Fold over the chicken to enclose the filling.

3 Brush the sheets of filo pastry lightly with oil. Sandwich together in pairs, then place a piece of chicken on each. Roll up the pastry, tucking in the ends to enclose the filling.

4 Place on a baking sheet and brush with oil, then sprinkle with poppy seeds. Bake in a preheated oven, 200°C/400°F/Gas Mark 6, for 30–35 minutes, until golden brown and bubbling. Cool on a wire rack. Serve with a tomato salad.

Sesame Chicken Pies

This chicken pie is easy to make with ready-made filo pastry. Thigh meat is very economical
and you can buy it ready diced, or just buy boneless thighs and chop them at home.

Serves 4
500g/1 lb diced chicken thigh meat
1 tbsp cornflour
250 g/8 oz/1 cup crème fraîche
1 tbsp chopped fresh chives
1 medium onion, thinly sliced
120 ml/4 fl oz/½ cup chicken stock
325 g/11 oz can sweetcorn (corn-on-the-cob), drained
4 sheets filo pastry
2 tbsp olive oil
1 tsp sesame seeds
salt and pepper

190°C/375°F/Gas Mark 5, for 50–60 minutes until golden (individual pies will take 30–35 minutes). Serve hot with a green vegetable.

COOK'S TIP

Packaged filo pastry is available fresh and frozen. It can be stored for up to 1 year in the freezer.

1 Toss the chicken in the cornflour to coat evenly. Stir in the crème fraîche and chives and season.

2 Place the onion in a pan with the chicken stock and simmer over a moderate heat, stirring until the onion is softened and most of the stock is evaporated. Add to the chicken with the sweetcorn.

3 Transfer the mixture to a large pie dish or divide among four 300 ml/½ pint ovenproof dishes. Place on a baking sheet.

4 Spread out the filo pastry and brush with oil.

5 Scrunch up the pastry to cover the filling of each pie. Sprinkle with sesame seeds.

6 Bake in a preheated oven,

Chicken wrapped in Puff Pastry with Lancashire Cheese & Mustard

This recipe is a variation on the classic Beef Wellington – and just as delicious.

Serves 6–8
500 g/1 lb chicken breast meat
45 g/1¹/₂ oz butter
2 onions, chopped finely
125 g/4 oz button mushrooms or wild mushrooms
2 ready-rolled sheets puff pastry
2 tbsp English mustard
125 g/4 oz chicken liver pâté
125 g/4 oz Lancashire cheese, crumbled
1 egg, lightly beaten
salt and pepper

1 With a sharp knife, trim the fat from the chicken and season well with salt and pepper.

2 Melt 2 tablespoons of butter in a large frying pan, add the chicken, and cook for about 4 minutes until sealed.

3 To the same pan, add the remaining butter and add the chopped onion and mushrooms. Cook until all the moisture has evaporated then allow to cool.

4 Roll out half of the pastry to a large rectangle and place on a greased baking sheet.

5 Spread the onion and mushroom mixture in the centre of the pastry and place the chicken on the mixture.

6 Top the chicken breasts with the mustard and liver pâté, then sprinkle them with a layer of the crumbled cheese.

7 Roll out the remaining pastry so it is slightly larger than the base.

8 Brush the edges of the pastry with egg then press together to seal.

9 Slash the top of the pastry with a sharp knife, then brush with egg.

10 Bake in the centre of a preheated oven, 200°C/400°F/Gas Mark 6, for 20 minutes, then lower the oven to 180°C/350°F/Gas Mark 4 for a further 20 minutes until golden brown.

Roast Chicken & Cranberry Pie

Cranberries are a good accompaniment to poultry
and make this pie very tasty, whether served hot or cold.

Serves 6
60 g/2 oz butter
2 leeks, sliced finely
8 shallots, sliced
125 g/4 oz mushrooms, sliced
30 g/1 oz plain flour
300 ml/ 1/2 pint milk, warmed
150 ml/1/4 pint double cream
500 g/1 lb roast chicken meat, diced
150 g/5 oz cranberry sauce
salt and pepper
175 g/6 oz shortcrust pastry for the base and 125 g/4 oz puff pastry for the top
1 egg, beaten, for glazing

1 Melt the butter in a large saucepan and gently fry the leeks, shallots and mushrooms for about 10 minutes, stirring occasionally.

2 Add the flour and cook for a further 2 minutes.

3 Gradually add the warm milk and cream, stirring continuously until the sauce becomes thick and creamy. Simmer for 2 minutes.

4 Add the chicken and cranberry sauce to the mixture.

5 Season well and allow the mixture to cool.

6 Roll out the shortcrust pastry for the base and use to line a greased ovenproof pie dish. Add the chicken mixture and top with the puff pastry.

Brush the top of the pie with the beaten egg. Bake in the centre of a preheated oven, 200°C/400°F/Gas Mark 6, for 30 minutes.

COOK'S TIP

Dried cranberries would make an interesting addition to the pie instead of the ready-made cranberry sauce.

Chicken, Cheese & Tarragon Pie

The best way to prepare this type of pie is to make
a shortcrust base with a puff pastry topping.

Serves 6
60 g/2 oz butter
2 carrots, diced finely
8 shallots, sliced
250 g/8 oz button mushrooms, sliced
30 g/1 oz plain flour
300 ml/½ pint milk, warmed
150 ml/¼ pint double cream
500 g/1 lb chicken breast, cooked and diced
3 tbsp chopped fresh tarragon
60 g/ 2 oz grated Cheddar cheese
salt and pepper
175 g/ 6 oz shortcrust pastry for the base and 125 g/4 oz puff pastry for the top
1 egg, for glazing

1 Melt the butter in a large saucepan and gently fry the carrots, shallots and button mushrooms for about 10 minutes, stirring occasionally.

2 Add the flour and cook for a further 2 minutes.

3 Gradually add the milk and cream, stirring continuously until the sauce becomes thick and creamy.

4 Simmer for 2 minutes.

5 Add the cooked chicken breast, tarragon and cheese to the sauce.

6 Season well and allow the mixture to cool.

7 Roll out the shortcrust pastry base and use to line a greased, oval ovenproof pie dish.

8 Add the chicken mixture and top with puff pastry. Brush with the beaten egg to glaze and bake in the centre of a preheated oven, 200°C/400°F/Gas Mark 6 for 30 minutes or until the top is golden.

9 Serve with garlic creamed potatoes and a green vegetable or salad.

Old Fashioned Chicken Pudding

This is a recipe from yesteryear made with suet pastry. Vegetable suet, which is made from hydrogenated vegetable oil is now an option if you don't want to use suet made from animal fat.

Serves 4
60 g/2 oz butter
pinch of fines herbes
4 skinless chicken breasts, sliced
90 g/3 oz button mushrooms
4 shallots, sliced
150 ml/$\frac{1}{4}$ pint fresh orange juice
1 sprig fresh thyme
4 tbsp brandy
150 ml$\frac{1}{4}$ pint game or chicken stock, thickened
250 g/8 oz suet pastry
salt and pepper

1 Melt the butter in a large frying pan, add the fines herbes, sliced chicken breasts, button mushrooms and shallots and pan-fry them for 6 minutes. Remove the breasts from the pan.

2 Add the orange juice, thyme, brandy and seasoning to the pan and simmer for at least 20 minutes until the liquid is reduced by half.

3 Add the game stock, simmer and again reduce by half.

4 Line a 20 cm/8 inch basin with suet pastry.

5 Put the meat and game stock into the basin.

6 Cover the top of the basin with suet pastry and press the pastry layers gently together to seal.

7 Brush the top with melted butter.

8 Cover the basin with several layers of cooking foil.

9 Steam the pudding in a covered saucepan for 2 hours, topping up the pan with extra water as necessary. Serve with fresh vegetables.

COOK'S TIP

Fines herbes is a classic mixture of parsley, chervil, tarragon and chives that is often used in French cooking.

Springtime Creamed Chicken & Vegetable Quiche

A quick-and-easy quiche that can be made even speedier
if you use ready-made pastry.

Serves 4–6
350 g/12 oz shortcrust pastry
30 g/1 oz butter
6 spring onions
125 g/4 oz leeks, shredded
125 g/4 oz button mushrooms
125 g/4 oz peas
175 g/6 oz grated Cheddar cheese
175 g/6 oz cooked chicken meat, sliced thinly
3 eggs
1 egg yolk
150 ml/$\frac{1}{4}$ pint each milk and double cream, mixed
salt and pepper

1 Roll out the pastry and use to line a 25 cm/10 inch fluted, loose-based flan tin.

2 Melt the butter in a large frying pan and fry the spring onions, leeks, mushrooms and peas over a low heat for 6 minutes.

3 Remove from the heat, sprinkle the base of the quiche with half of the cheese then add the chicken and vegetables.

4 Finish with the remaining cheese.

5 Beat the eggs and egg yolk and the milk and cream mixture together and pour over the chicken and vegetables.

6 Bake in the centre of a preheated oven, 190°C/375°F/Gas Mark 5, for 35–45 minutes until the filling is set and golden brown.

COOK'S VARIATION

If you prefer, substitute single cream
for the milk and cream mixture.

Savoury Criss Cross

This is a very tasty picnic bake which can be served hot or cold.
Try serving it with home-made ginger beer.

Serves 6
350 g/12 oz ready-made shortcrust pastry
3 large hard-boiled eggs, sliced
8 slices lean, rindless streaky bacon, grilled and chopped
250 g/8 oz cooked chicken, diced
250 g/8 oz sausage meat
1 egg beaten with 150 ml/¼ pint milk
salt and pepper

1 Roll out two-thirds of the pastry and use to line a buttered pie dish or a deep plate.

2 Arrange the eggs, bacon, chicken and sausage meat in the pastry case.

3 Pour over the egg and milk mixture.

4 Season well. Roll out the remaining pastry and cut into thin strips about 1 cm/½ inch wide, and lay them across the pie in a criss-cross pattern. Seal well all around the edges.

5 Bake in the centre of a preheated oven, 200°C/400°F/Gas Mark 6, for 10 minutes. Reduce the heat to 180°C/350°F/Gas Mark 4, and bake for a further 25 minutes.

COOK'S TIP

Use your favourite sausages in this recipe – simply remove and discard the sausage skins, then loosen the sausage meat with a fork.

Terrine of Chicken & Ham with Cranberry & Shallot Marmalade

This is a very impressive terrine that would be suitable for any special occasion.
The cranberry and shallot marmalade is a perfect accompaniment.

Serves 6–8
500 g/1 lb chicken meat, roughly chopped
120 ml/4 fl oz sherry
250 g/8 oz minced pork
1 small onion, chopped
3 eggs, beaten
500 g/1 lb lean cooked ham, diced
500 g/1 lb rindless streaky bacon

CRANBERRY & SHALLOT MARMALADE

2 onions, chopped
30 g/1 oz butter
4 tbsp cranberries
1 tbsp brown sugar
8 shallots, chopped
salt and pepper

1 Remove any fat or sinews from the chicken meat, place it in a bowl with the sherry, and marinate for 3 hours. Add the pork, onion and the eggs. Season and mix thoroughly.

2 Mix the pieces of ham into the mixture.

3 Line a 1.2 litre/2 pint ovenproof terrine dish with the bacon slices.

4 Add the chicken mixture, top with the remaining bacon, then cover with greased cooking foil.

5 Bake in the centre of a preheated oven, 180°C/350°F/Gas Mark 4, for 1½ hours. Remove the foil and allow to cool naturally, then chill for at least 4 hours before serving.

6 For the cranberry and shallot marmalade, fry the onions gently for 2 minutes in the butter. Season.

7 Add the cranberries, brown sugar and shallots and cook for 5 minutes. Pour some cranberry and shallot marmalade onto individual plates and serve with a generous slice of the terrine. Garnish with orange slices and fresh bread.

Potted Chicken & Cheese Terrine

Make this terrine at least two weeks before using it. This allows all the
wonderful flavours of the cheeses, chicken, spices and sherry to blend together
and mellow. Serve with warm oat cakes and a good port.

Serves 4
125 g/4 oz Wensleydale cheese
125 g/4 oz Lancashire cheese
350 g/12 oz cooked chicken fillet, shredded
125 g/4 oz butter
1 tbsp English mustard
150 ml/¼ pint cream sherry
large pinch of mace
pinch of cayenne pepper
250 g/8 oz butter

1 Crumble or grate the cheeses and place all the ingredients except the butter into a blender or food processor. Mix thoroughly, while slowly adding the sherry.

2 Place into individual ramekins and make the clarified butter.

3 Place the butter in a small saucepan and heat very gently, skimming off the foam as the butter heats.

4 Stand for 5 minutes then strain the butter through muslin into a bowl.

5 Pour the clarified butter over the mixture in the ramekins and leave to cool, then chill.

COOK'S TIP

Because the milk solids are not present in clarified butter, it keeps better than ordinary, unheated butter.

Chicken, Basil & Walnut Terrine

A terrine is a chunky pâté, which takes its name from the deep rectangular dish in which it is baked. If you don't have a terrine, a loaf tin can be used instead. This moist, basil-flavoured dish is ideal for summer meals and picnics, served with a simple salad.

Serves 6
250 g/8 oz streaky bacon
750 g/1½ lb skinless, boneless chicken thighs
280 g/9 oz cream cheese or ricotta
15 g/½ oz fresh basil leaves
1 tbsp sunflower oil
1 small onion, chopped finely
15 g/½ oz butter
200 g/7 oz chicken livers, chopped
90 g/3 oz mushrooms, chopped
45 g/1½ oz walnuts, chopped
salt and pepper
sautéed mushrooms, to garnish

1 Stretch the bacon with the back of a knife and use to line a 1.75 litre/3 pint terrine dish or loaf tin.

2 Place one-third of the chicken, the cream cheese and the basil in a food processor and blend until almost smooth. Season well.

3 Heat the oil and fry the onion gently to soften. Finely chop the rest of the chicken and add to the pan, stirring until lightly coloured but not browned. Remove from the heat, stir in the cheese mixture and season the mixture well.

4 Spoon half the mixture into the terrine dish, smoothing the top until it is level.

5 Melt the butter and fry the chicken livers and mushrooms for 3–4 minutes, stirring until the chicken is lightly coloured.

6 Add the walnuts and spoon evenly over the chicken mixture. Top with the remaining chicken mixture.

7 Cover with a lid or foil and bake in a preheated oven, 180°C/350°F/Gas Mark 4, for 1–1¼ hours, or until there is no trace of pink juices. Remove from the oven and place a weight on top. Leave to cool completely before turning out, or serve straight from the terrine dish. Garnish with sautéed mushrooms and serve in slices, with salad and French bread.

Chicken & Mushroom Terrine

This terrine is extremely quick to make if you use a food processor.
Sunflower seeds add a pleasing crunchy texture.

Serves 4
1 tbsp oil
500 g/1 lb skinless, boneless chicken breasts, roughly chopped
250 g/8 oz mushrooms
1 medium onion, quartered
1 garlic clove, crushed
30 g/1 oz fresh brown breadcrumbs
3 tbsp chopped fresh parsley
3 tbsp chopped fresh sage
30 g/1 oz/2 tbsp sunflower seeds
salt and pepper

1 Brush a 1 litre/1¾ pint terrine dish or loaf tin with half of the oil.

2 Place the chicken, mushrooms and onion in a food processor and process until finely chopped.

3 Add the garlic, breadcrumbs, herbs and sunflower seeds, then season with salt and pepper.

4 Spoon the chicken mixture into the terrine and press down.

5 Brush with the remaining oil and loosely cover with foil. Bake in a preheated oven, 350°C/180°F/Gas Mark 4, for about 50 minutes, or until the juices run clear when the terrine is pierced with a skewer. Cool in the terrine then serve in thick slices with crusty bread.

Barbecues & Grills

There is nothing more delicious than the juicy flesh and charred skin of chicken that has been grilled over an open fire – after marinating in a flavourful mixture of oil and herbs or spices. Try an Asian-style mixture of yogurt and aromatic spices, or soy sauce, sesame oil and fresh ginger root, or a Cajun-inspired marinade of warm spices and garlic for Blackened Chicken with Guacamole. In this section, chicken comes in all shapes and sizes, it is minced to make Lemon & Mint Chicken Burgers, spatchcocked for Barbecued Chicken and cut into tiny, bite-sized pieces for Spicy Chicken Tikka. There are some unusual flavours and innovative tastes, including Skewered Chicken with Bramble Sauce, and Skewered Chicken Spirals, which are attractive whirls of chicken, bacon and basil. Baby chickens, flavoured with lemon and tarragon in this section, are perfect for grilling or barbecuing.

Lemon & Mint Chicken Burgers

Use chicken leg meat for these delicious burgers – it has
much more flavour than breast meat.

Serves 4
750 g/1¹/₂ lb minced chicken leg meat
4 tbsp chopped fresh mint
grated rind of 1 lemon
juice of 1 lemon
olive oil
90 g/3 oz pitted black olives, chopped
1 round focaccia bread, either plain or flavoured
lettuce leaf and lemon slices, to garnish
salt
lemon pepper (or black pepper)

1 In a large bowl, combine the chicken, mint, lemon rind, lemon juice, 1 tablespoon of olive oil, black olives, salt and lemon pepper. Leave to marinade for at least 2 hours.

2 Form the mixture into four patties, eliminating any air holes by pressing between your hands. Return to the refrigerator until ready to serve.

3 When ready to serve, cut the foccacia into four quarters, halve and brush each half with olive oil liberally, and toast under a grill – do not use a toaster.

4 Fry the chicken patties in a little olive oil, for about 10 minutes, until cooked through. Remove the patties with a perforated spoon and drain on paper towels. Put each patty between two pieces of bread, and serve.

Chicken in Spicy Yogurt

Make sure the barbecue is really hot before you start cooking.
The coals should be white and glow red when fanned. You could also cook
the chicken under a very hot preheated grill (broiler).

Serves 6
3 dried red chillies
2 tbsp coriander seed
2 tsp turmeric
2 tsp garam masala
4 garlic cloves, crushed
1/2 onion, chopped
2.5cm/1 inch piece fresh ginger root, grated
2 tbsp lime juice
1 tsp salt
120 ml/4 fl oz natural yogurt
1 tbsp oil
2 kg/4 lb chicken, cut into 6 pieces, or 6 chicken portions

TO SERVE

chopped tomatoes
diced cucumber
sliced red onion
cucumber and yogurt

1 Grind together the chillies, coriander seed, turmeric, garam masala, garlic, onion, ginger, lime juice and salt with a pestle and mortar or grinder.

2 Gently heat a frying pan and add the spice paste. Stir until fragrant, about 2 minutes. Turn into a shallow non-porous dish.

3 Add the yogurt to the spice paste and oil, and mix well to combine.

4 Remove the skin from the chicken portions and make three slashes in the flesh of each piece. Add the chicken to the dish and make sure that the pieces are coated completely in the marinade. Cover and chill for at least 4 hours. Remove the dish from the refrigerator and leave covered at room temperature for 30 minutes before cooking.

5 Wrap the chicken pieces in foil, sealing well so the juices cannot escape. Cook the chicken pieces over a very hot barbecue for about 15 minutes, turning once.

6 Remove the foil, with tongs, and brown the chicken on the barbecue for 5 minutes. Serve with the chopped tomatoes, diced cucumber, sliced red onion and yogurt mixture.

Chargrilled Chicken Salad

This is a quick dish to serve at a barbecue while your hungry guests are waiting for the main event. If the bread is bent in half, the chicken salad can be put in the middle
and eaten as finger food – remember to provide napkins!

Serves 4
2 skinless, boneless chicken breasts
1 red onion
oil for brushing
1 avocado, peeled and pitted
1 tbsp lemon juice
120 ml/4 fl oz mayonnaise
$^1/_4$ tsp chilli powder
$^1/_2$ tsp pepper
$^1/_4$ tsp salt
4 tomatoes, quartered
$^1/_2$ loaf sun-dried tomato-flavoured focaccia bread
green salad, to serve

1 Cut the chicken breasts into 1 cm/$^1/_2$ inch strips.

2 Cut the onion into eight pieces, held together at the root. Rinse under cold running water and then brush with oil.

3 Purée or mash the avocado and lemon juice together. Whisk in the mayonnaise. Add the chilli powder, pepper and salt.

4 Put the chicken and onion over a hot barbecue and grill for 3–4 minutes on each side.

5 Combine the chicken, onion, tomatoes and avocado mixture together.

6 Cut the bread in half twice, so that you have quarter-circle-shaped pieces,

then in half horizontally. Toast on the hot barbecue for about 2 minutes on each side.

7 Spoon the chicken mixture on top of the toasts and serve at once with a green salad.

Spicy Chicken Tikka

Arrange these tasty kebabs on a bed of finely shredded crisp lettuce, sliced onion
and grated eating apple, drizzled with a little lemon or lime juice.

Serves 6
500 g/1 lb skinless, boneless chicken breasts
1¹/₂ tbsp Tikka paste (from a jar)
6 tbsp thick natural yogurt
1 tbsp lemon juice
¹/₂ onion, chopped finely
1¹/₂ tbsp chopped fresh chives or spring onion tops
1¹/₂ tbsp finely chopped fresh ginger root
1–2 garlic cloves, crushed
1¹/₂ tbsp sesame seeds
2 tbsp vegetable oil
salt and pepper
wedges of lemon or lime, to garnish

1 Cut the chicken breasts into small bite-sized pieces, place in a shallow glass dish, and season with salt and pepper to taste.

2 In a small bowl, mix together the remaining ingredients, except the sesame seeds and oil, and pour over the chicken. Mix well until all the chicken pieces are coated, then cover and refrigerate for at least 1 hour, or for longer if possible.

3 Thread the chicken pieces on to six bamboo or metal skewers and sprinkle with the sesame seeds.

4 Place on a rack in a grill pan and drizzle with the oil. Cook under a hot grill for about 15 minutes or until cooked through and browned, turning frequently and brushing with more oil, if necessary. Serve hot, garnished with wedges of lemon or lime.

COOK'S TIP

Don't place the kebabs too near to the heat or the sesame seeds will burn before the chicken is cooked.

Sesame Skewered Chicken with Ginger Baste

Chunks of chicken breast are marinated in a mixture of lime juice, garlic, sesame oil and fresh ginger to give them a spicy, aromatic flavour.

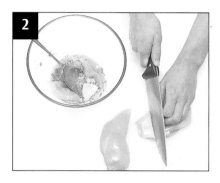

Serves 4
500 g/1 lb boneless chicken breasts
sprigs of fresh mint, to garnish

MARINADE
1 garlic clove, crushed
1 shallot, chopped very finely
2 tbsp sesame oil
1 tbsp fish sauce or light soy sauce
finely grated rind of 1 lime or 1/2 lemon
2 tbsp lime juice or lemon juice
1 tsp sesame seeds
2 tsp finely grated fresh ginger root
2 tsp chopped fresh mint
salt and pepper

1 To make the marinade, put the garlic, shallot, sesame oil, fish sauce or soy sauce, lime or lemon rind and juice, sesame seeds, ginger and chopped mint into a large non-metallic bowl. Season to taste with a little salt and pepper.

2 Remove the skin from the chicken breasts and cut the flesh into chunks. Add them to the marinade, stirring to coat them in the mixture. Cover and chill for at least 2 hours. Soak four wooden satay sticks in warm water for 30 minutes

3 Thread the chicken on to the wooden satay sticks. Place them on the rack of a grill pan and baste with the marinade.

4 Place the kebabs under a preheated grill for about 8–10 minutes. Turn them frequently, basting with the remaining marinade.

5 Serve at once, garnished with sprigs of fresh mint.

Blackened Chicken with Guacamole

This easy recipe is typical of French Cajun cooking which has its roots in earthy, strong flavours, and uses plenty of spice. The dish includes a typical Cajun spice mix.

Serves 4
4 skinless boneless chicken breasts
60 g/2 oz butter, melted

SPICE MIX
1 tsp salt
1 tbsp sweet paprika
1 tsp dried onion granules
1 tsp dried garlic granules
1 tsp dried thyme
1 tsp cayenne
$^1/_2$ tsp cracked black pepper
$^1/_2$ tsp dried oregano

GUACAMOLE
1 avocado
1 tbsp lemon juice
2 tbsp soured cream
$^1/_2$ red onion, chopped
1 garlic clove, halved

1 Put each chicken breast between two pieces of clingfilm, and pound with a mallet or rolling pin until it is an even thickness. It should be about 1 cm/½ inch thick.

2 Brush each chicken breast all over with the melted butter. Set aside.

3 Combine the spice mix ingredients in a shallow bowl.

4 Coat the chicken breasts with the spice mix, ensuring that they are covered completely. Set aside.

5 To make the guacamole, mash the avocado thoroughly with the lemon juice in a small bowl. Stir in the soured cream and red onion.

6 Wipe the garlic clove around the guacamole serving dish, pressing hard. Spoon in the guacamole.

7 Place the chicken breasts over the hottest part of a very hot barbecue and cook for 8–10 minutes, turning once.

8 Slice the breasts into thick pieces and serve immediately with the guacamole.

Jerk Chicken

This is a popular Caribbean dish. Rubbing pastes and 'rubs' into meat, poultry, fish or seafood is an old method of cooking introduced by the Arawak Indians that helps to tenderize the meat.

Serves 6
1.5 kg/3 lb chicken pieces
cherry tomatoes, to garnish
salad, to serve
MARINADE
6 spring onions
2 fresh red chillies, preferably Scotch bonnet
2 tbsp dark soy sauce
2 tbsp lime juice
3 tsp ground allspice
½ tsp ground bay leaves
1 tsp ground cinnamon
2 garlic cloves, chopped
2 tsp brown sugar
1 tsp dried thyme
½ tsp salt

1 To make the marinade, chop the spring onions. Deseed and finely chop the chillies. Put the spring onions, chillies, soy sauce, lime juice, allspice, ground bay leaves, cinnamon, garlic, sugar, thyme and salt in a food processor or blender and blend until smooth. Alternatively, finely chop the spring onions and chillies (being careful not to touch your eyes) add these to the remaining ingredients and, using a pestle and mortar, work to a chunky paste.

2 Place the chicken in a shallow dish and generously spoon over the marinade. Cover and leave in the refrigerator to marinate for 24 hours, turning each piece of chicken several times in the marinade.

3 Brush a grill rack with oil and place the chicken on it. Grill under a preheated medium grill for about 15–20 minutes on each side until the chicken juices run clear when the thickest part of each piece is pierced with a sharp knife.

4 Garnish with cherry tomatoes and serve with a salad.

Filipino Chicken

This recipe is from the Philippines. Tomato ketchup is a very popular
ingredient in Asian dishes, as it has a tangy, sweet-sour flavour.

Serves 4

1 can lemonade or
lime-and-lemonade
2 tbsp gin
4 tbsp tomato ketchup
2 tsp garlic salt
2 tsp Worcestershire sauce
4 chicken supremes
or breast fillets
salt and pepper

TO SERVE

thread egg noodles
1 green chilli, chopped finely
2 spring onions,
sliced

6 Serve the chicken with egg noodles,
tossed with a little green chilli and
spring onion.

COOK'S TIP

Wash your hands after handling chillies
as their fiery seeds and flesh can cause
painful burning.

1 Combine the lemonade or lime-
and-lemonade, gin, tomato ketchup,
garlic salt, Worcestershire sauce and
seasoning in a large non-porous dish.

2 Put the chicken supremes into the
dish. Cover the chicken completely
with the marinade.

3 Leave to marinate in the
refrigerator for 2 hours. Remove and
leave, covered, at room temperature
for 30 minutes.

4 Place the chicken over a medium
barbecue and cook for 20 minutes.
Turn the chicken once, halfway
through the cooking time.

5 Remove from the barbecue and
leave to rest for 3–4 minutes before
serving.

Thai Chicken with Peanut Sauce

A favourite Thai dish, served with a spicy peanut sauce. that
can be made with chicken or beef.

Serves 4–6

4 skinless, boneless chicken breasts

MARINADE

1 small onion, finely chopped
1 garlic clove, crushed
2.5 cm/1 inch piece fresh
ginger root,
2 tbsp dark soy sauce
2 tsp chilli powder
1 tsp ground coriander seeds
2 tsp dark brown sugar
1 tbsp lemon or lime juice
1 tbsp vegetable oil

SPICY PEANUT SAUCE

300 ml/$^1/_2$ pint
coconut milk
4 tbsp/$^1/_3$ cup crunchy
peanut butter
1 tbsp fish sauce
1 tsp lemon or lime juice
salt and pepper

1 Trim any fat from the chicken
breasts then cut into thin strips,
about 7 cm/3 inches long.

2 To make the marinade, place all the
ingredients in a shallow dish and mix
well. Add the chicken strips and turn
in the marinade until well coated.
Cover and put in the refrigerator to
marinate for 2 hours or overnight.

3 Remove the chicken from the
marinade and thread the pieces,
concertina style, on bamboo or thin
wooden skewers.

4 Grill for 8–10 minutes, turning and
brushing occasionally with the
marinade, until cooked.

5 Meanwhile, to make the spicy
peanut sauce, mix the coconut milk

with the peanut butter, fish sauce and
lemon or lime juice in a pan. Bring to
the boil and cook for 3 minutes.
Season with salt and pepper to taste
and serve the sauce with the cooked
chicken satay.

Chicken Satay Kebabs

Small kebabs of satay chicken with cubes of cheese and cherry tomatoes
are served on crisp lettuce leaves.

Serves 8
1 tbsp sherry
1 tbsp light soy sauce
1 tbsp sesame oil
finely grated rind of $1/2$ lemon
1 tbsp lemon or lime juice
2 tsp sesame seeds
500 g/1 lb skinless, boneless chicken breasts
90 g/3 oz Double Gloucester cheese or Gouda cheese
16 cherry tomatoes
crisp lettuce leaves, such as Little Gem
salt and pepper

PEANUT DIP

30 g/1 oz desiccated coconut
150 ml/$1/4$ pint boiling water
125 g/4 oz crunchy peanut butter
good pinch of chilli powder
1 tsp brown sugar
1 tbsp light soy sauce
2 spring onions, trimmed and chopped

1 Combine the sherry, soy sauce, sesame oil, lemon rind, lemon or lime juice, sesame seeds, and salt and pepper in a bowl.

2 Cut the chicken into 2.5 cm/1 inch cubes. Add to the marinade and mix well. Cover and chill for 3–6 hours.

3 To make the dip, put the coconut in a saucepan with the boiling water and bring back to the boil. Leave until cold.

4 Add the peanut butter, chilli powder, sugar and soy sauce and bring slowly to the boil. Simmer gently, stirring, for 2–3 minutes until thickened, then cool.

5 Soak eight wooden skewers in warm water for 30 minutes. When the mixture is cold, stir in the spring onions. Turn into a bowl.

6 Thread the chicken on to eight wooden skewers. Cook under a moderate grill for about 5 minutes on each side until cooked through. Leave until cold.

7 Cut the cheese into 16 cubes and add a cube and a cherry tomato to each end of the skewers.

8 Serve on lettuce with the dip.

Sticky Chicken Wings

These need to be eaten with your fingers so serve
them at an informal supper.

Serves 4–6

1 small onion, finely chopped
2 garlic cloves, crushed
2 tbsp olive oil
450 ml/³/₄ pint tomato passata
2 tsp dried thyme
1 tsp dried oregano
pinch fennel seeds
3 tbsp red wine vinegar
2 tbsp Dijon mustard
pinch ground cinnamon
2 tbsp brown sugar
1 tsp chilli flakes
2 tbsp black treacle
16 chicken wings
salt and pepper

1 Soften the onion and garlic in the oil for about 10 minutes.

2 Add the passata, dried herbs, fennel seeds, vinegar, mustard and cinnamon to the pan with the sugar, chilli flakes, treacle, and salt and pepper. Bring to the boil, then reduce the heat and simmer gently for 15 minutes or so, until slightly reduced.

3 Put the chicken wings in a large dish, and coat liberally with the sauce. Marinade for 3 hours or as long as possible, stirring often.

4 Transfer the wings to a clean baking sheet, and roast in a preheated oven, 220°C/425°F/Gas Mark 7, for 10 minutes. Reduce the heat to 190°C/375°F/Gas Mark 5 and cook for 20 minutes, basting often.

5 Serve piping hot with celery sticks and cherry tomatoes.

COOK'S VARIATION

Instead of black treacle, use either honey or maple syrup for a different flavour and lighter colour.

Crispy-Coated Baby Chickens

You could adapt this recipe using a whole chicken or chicken pieces,
serving them on a bed of moist and colourful vegetables.

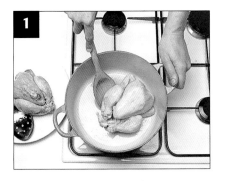

Serves 6
4 tbsp vegetable oil
60 g/2 oz butter
6 small baby chickens, trussed
1 large onion, sliced
500 g/1 lb baby carrots
1 tbsp flour
150 ml/¹⁄₄ pint white wine
juice of 2 oranges
2 fennel bulbs, quartered
300 ml/¹⁄₂ pint chicken stock
¹⁄₂ tsp salt
1 tbsp black peppercorns, lightly crushed
1 tsp cornflour
150 ml/¹⁄₄ pint thick natural yogurt
salt and pepper

COATING

3 tbsp demerara sugar
1 tbsp black peppercorns, lightly crushed
3 tbsp coarse sea salt
150 ml/¹⁄₄ pint thick natural yogurt

1 Heat the oil in a large frying pan and add the butter. When bubbling, add the baby chickens in batches until golden. Remove and keep warm.

2 Add the onion to the pan and fry until translucent. Add the carrots, stir, then sprinkle with the flour and blend well. Add the wine and orange juice while stirring. Add the fennel, stock, salt and peppercorns. Bring to the boil then pour into a roasting tin.

3 Arrange the baby chickens in the roasting tin, cover with foil and cook in the oven for 40 minutes.

4 To make the coating, stir together the sugar, peppercorns, salt and yogurt to make a thick paste.

5 Preheat the grill to high. Remove the baby chickens from the roasting tin and place them on a rack. Spread the paste evenly over the baby chickens then grill for 3–4 minutes, until the coating is crisp.

6 Arrange the drained vegetables on a warm serving dish. Place the roasting tin over medium heat and bring the sauce to the boil. Stir the cornflour into the yogurt then blend into the sauce. Taste for seasoning. Place the baby chickens in the centre of the dish, spoon a little sauce over the vegetables, and serve the rest separately.

Grilled Chicken Salad

Grilling is a quick, healthy cooking method, ideal for sealing in the juices and flavour of chicken breasts, and a wonderful way to cook summer vegetables. Choose a good quality olive oil to enhance the fresh flavours to the full.

Serves 4
1 small aubergine, sliced
2 garlic cloves, crushed
finely grated rind of $\frac{1}{2}$ lemon
1 tbsp chopped fresh mint
6 tbsp olive oil
4 boneless chicken breasts
2 medium courgettes, sliced
1 medium red pepper, quartered
1 small bulb fennel, sliced thickly
1 large red onion, sliced thickly
1 small ciabatta loaf or 1 French baguette, sliced
extra olive oil
salt and pepper

they are golden brown and tender, or cook on a ridged griddle pan on the hob. Brush the bread slices with olive oil and grill until golden.

5 Drizzle a little olive oil over the chicken and grilled vegetables and serve hot or cold with the crusty bread toasts and a salad.

1 Place the aubergine slices in a colander and sprinkle with salt. Leave over a bowl to drain for 30 minutes, then rinse and dry. Mix together the garlic, lemon rind, mint, and olive oil and season.

2 Slash the chicken breasts at intervals with a sharp knife. Spoon over about half of the oil mixture.

3 Combine the aubergines and the remaining vegetables, then toss in the remaining oil mixture. Marinate the chicken and vegetables for about 30 minutes.

4 Place the chicken breasts and vegetables on a preheated hot grill or barbecue, turning occasionally, until

Mustardy Barbecue Drummers

Great for barbecues, or for simple summer lunches and picnics,
this is an easy and tasty recipe for chicken drumsticks.

Serves 4
10 slices smoked streaky bacon
1 garlic clove, peeled and crushed
3 tbsp wholegrain mustard
4 tbsp fresh brown breadcrumbs
8 chicken drumsticks
1 tbsp sunflower oil

1 Chop and fry two of the bacon slices without fat for 3–4 minutes, stirring. Remove from the heat and stir in the garlic, 2 tablespoons of mustard and the breadcrumbs.

2 Carefully loosen the skin from each drumstick. Spoon a little of the mustard stuffing under each, smoothing over firmly.

3 Wrap a bacon rasher around each drumstick, and secure with cocktail sticks.

4 Mix together the remaining mustard and the oil, brush over the chicken and cook on a preheated moderately hot barbecue or grill for about 25 minutes, until there is no trace of pink in the chicken juices when pierced with a skewer. Serve hot or cold.

COOK'S TIP

Don't cook the chicken over the hottest part of the barbecue or the outside may be charred before the centre is cooked.

Skewered Spicy Tomato Chicken

These low-fat, spicy skewers are cooked in a matter of minutes – and they can be assembled ahead of time and stored in the fridge until you need them.

Serves 4

500 g/1 lb skinless, boneless
chicken breasts
3 tbsp tomato purée
2 tbsp clear honey
2 tbsp Worcestershire sauce
1 tbsp chopped fresh rosemary
250 g/8 oz cherry tomatoes
sprigs of rosemary,
to garnish

1 Cut the chicken into 2.5 cm/1 inch chunks and place in a bowl.

2 Mix together the tomato purée, honey, Worcestershire sauce and rosemary. Add to the chicken, stirring to coat evenly.

3 Alternating the chicken pieces and tomatoes, thread them onto eight wooden skewers.

4 Spoon over any remaining glaze. Cook under a preheated hot grill for 8–10 minutes, turning occasionally, until the chicken is thoroughly cooked. Serve on a bed of couscous or rice and garnish with sprigs of rosemary.

COOK'S TIP

Couscous is made from semolina that has been made into separate grains. It usually just needs moistening or steaming before serving.

Barbecued Chicken Quarters with Warm Aioli

Chicken quarters are barbecued then served with a strongly flavoured garlic mayonnaise, which originated in Provence, France.

Serves 4

4 chicken quarters
2 tbsp oil
2 tbsp lemon juice
2 tsp dried thyme
salt and pepper

AIOLI

5 garlic cloves, crushed
2 egg yolks
120 ml/4 fl oz each
olive oil and sunflower oil
2 tsp lemon juice
2 tbsp boiling water

1 Using a skewer, prick the chicken quarters in several places then place them in a shallow dish.

2 Mix the oil, lemon juice, thyme and seasoning together, then pour over the chicken. Turn the chicken quarters to ensure they are well coated with the marinade. Set aside for 2 hours.

3 To make the aioli, put the garlic in a bowl with a pinch of salt and beat together to make a paste. Add the egg yolks and beat well. Gradually add the oils, drop by drop, beating vigorously, until the mayonnaise becomes creamy and smooth. Add the oils in a thin steady trickle and continue beating until the aioli is thick. Stir in the lemon juice and season with pepper. Set aside in a warm place.

4 Place the chicken on a preheated barbecue and cook for about 25–30 minutes. Brush with the marinade and turn the portions so that they cook evenly. Remove and arrange on a serving plate.

5 Beat the water into the aioli and turn into a warmed serving bowl. Serve with the chicken.

COOK'S TIP

To make a quick aioli, add the garlic to 300 ml/½ pint good quality mayonnaise then place in a bowl over a pan of warm water and beat together. Just before serving add 1–2 tablespoons of hot water.

Skewered Chicken with Bramble Sauce

This autumnal recipe can be made with fresh-picked wild blackberries from the hedgerow if you're lucky enough to have a good supply.

Serves 4
4 chicken breasts or 8 thighs
4 tbsp dry white wine or cider
2 tbsp chopped fresh rosemary
pepper
rosemary sprigs
and blackberries, to garnish

SAUCE
200 g/7 oz
blackberries
1 tbsp cider vinegar
2 tbsp redcurrant jelly
$^1/_4$ tsp grated nutmeg

1 Cut the chicken into 2.5cm/1 inch pieces and place in a bowl. Sprinkle over the wine and rosemary, and season well with pepper. Cover and leave to marinate for at least an hour.

2 Drain the marinade from the chicken and thread the meat onto 8 metal or wooden skewers.

3 Cook on a preheated moderately hot grill for 8–10 minutes, turning occasionally, until golden and evenly cooked.

4 Meanwhile, to make the sauce, place the marinade in a pan with the blackberries and simmer gently until soft. Press though a sieve.

5 Return to the pan with the cider vinegar and redcurrant jelly and bring to the boil. Boil uncovered until the sauce is reduced by about one-third.

6 Spoon a little bramble sauce onto each plate and place a chicken skewer on top. Sprinkle with nutmeg and serve hot. Garnish with rosemary and blackberries.

COOK'S TIP

If you use canned fruit, omit the redcurrant jelly.

Chicken Cajun-Style

These spicy chicken wings are good served with a chilli salsa and salad.

Serves 4
16 chicken wings
4 tsp paprika
2 tsp ground coriander
1 tsp celery salt
1 tsp ground cumin
$1/2$ tsp cayenne
$1/2$ tsp salt
1 tbsp oil
2 tbsp red wine vinegar

1 Wash and dry the chicken wings and remove the wing tips.

2 Mix together the paprika, coriander, celery salt, cumin, cayenne, the salt, oil and vinegar.

3 Rub this mixture over the wings and set aside, in the refrigerator, for a least 1 hour to allow the flavours to permeate the chicken.

4 Cook the wings on a preheated barbecue, occasionally brushing with oil, for about 15 minutes, turning often until cooked through.

COOK'S TIP

To save time, you can buy ready-made Cajun spice seasoning to rub over the chicken wings.

Chicken with Garden Herbs

Warm weather calls for lighter eating, and this chilled chicken dish in a subtle herb vinaigrette is ideal for a summer dinner party, or for a picnic. The chicken can be cooked several hours before you need it and stored in the fridge until required.

Serves 4
4 part-boned, skinless chicken breasts
6 tbsp olive oil
2 tbsp lemon juice
4 tbsp finely chopped summer herbs, such as parsley, chives and mint
1 ripe avocado
125 g/4 oz low-fat fromage frais
pepper

1 Using a sharp knife, cut 3–4 deep slashes in the chicken breasts.

2 Place in a flameproof dish and brush lightly with a little of the olive oil. Cook the chicken on a preheated moderately hot grill turning once until golden and the juices run clear when the chicken is pierced with a skewer.

3 Combine the remaining oil with the lemon juice and herbs and season with pepper. Spoon the oil over the chicken and leave to cool. Chill for at least 1 hour.

4 Mash the avocado or purée in a food processor with the fromage frais. Season with pepper to taste. Serve the chicken with the avocado sauce.

Ginger Chicken & Corn

Chicken wings and corn in a sticky ginger marinade are designed to be eaten
with the fingers – there's no other way! The corn has a delicious nutty texture,
and if fresh corn is unavailable, you can use thawed, frozen corn instead.

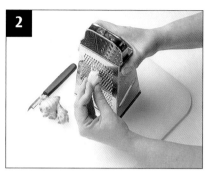

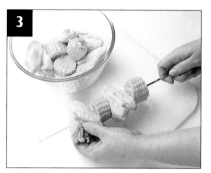

Serves 6
3 cobs fresh sweetcorn
12 chicken wings
2.5cm/1in piece fresh ginger root
6 tbsp lemon juice
4 tsp sunflower oil
1 tbsp golden caster sugar

1 Remove the husks and silks from the corn and cut each cob into 6 slices. Place in a large bowl with the chicken wings.

2 Peel and grate the ginger or chop finely. Mix together with the lemon juice, oil and sugar, then toss with the corn and chicken to coat.

3 Thread the corn and wings onto skewers, to make turning easier.

4 Cook under a preheated moderately hot grill or barbecue for 15–20 minutes, basting with the gingery glaze and turning frequently until the corn is golden brown and tender and the chicken is cooked. Serve with jacket potatoes or salad.

COOK'S TIP

Cut off the wing tips before grilling as they burn very easily. Or you can cover them with small pieces of foil.

Skewered Chicken Spirals

These unusual chicken kebabs have a wonderful Mediterranean flavour, and the bacon helps keep them moist during cooking. They are quite easy to assemble, and can be made earlier in the day and refrigerated until needed.

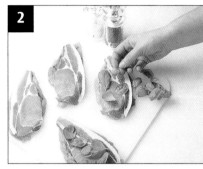

Serves 4
4 skinless, boneless chicken breasts
1 garlic clove, crushed
2 tbsp tomato purée
4 slices smoked back bacon
large handful fresh basil leaves
oil for brushing
salt and pepper

1 Spread out a piece of chicken between two sheets of cling film and beat firmly with a rolling pin to flatten the chicken to an even thickness. Repeat with the remaining chicken.

2 Mix the garlic and tomato purée and spread over the chicken. Lay a bacon slice over each, then scatter with the fresh basil. Season well with salt and pepper.

3 Roll up each piece of chicken firmly, then cut into thick slices.

4 Thread the slices onto four skewers, making sure the skewer holds the chicken in a spiral shape.

5 Brush lightly with oil and cook on a preheated hot barbecue or grill for about 10 minutes, turning once. Serve hot with a green salad.

Tropical Chicken Skewers

Chicken is given a Caribbean flavour. The marinade keeps them
moist and succulent during cooking.

Serves 6
750 g/1½ lb boneless chicken breasts
2 tbsp medium sherry
3 mangoes
bay leaves
2 tbsp oil
2 tbsp coarsely shredded coconut
pepper

1 Cut the chicken into 2.5 cm/1 inch cubes and toss in the sherry, with a little pepper.

2 Cut the mangoes into 2.5 cm/1 inch cubes, discarding the stone and skin.

3 Thread the chicken, mango cubes and bay leaves alternately onto long skewers, then brush lightly with oil.

4 Grill the skewers on a preheated moderately hot grill for 8–10 minutes, turning occasionally until golden. Sprinkle with the coconut and grill for a further 30 seconds. Serve the kebabs hot with a crisp green salad.

COOK'S TIP

Use mangoes that are ripe but still firm so that they hold together on the skewers during cooking. Another firm fruit that would be suitable is pineapple.

Spicy Sesame Chicken

This is a quick and easy recipe for the grill, perfect
for lunch or to eat outdoors on a picnic.

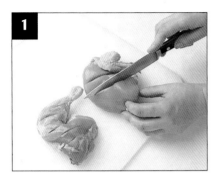  

Serves 4
4 chicken quarters
150 g/5 oz natural yogurt
finely grated rind and juice of 1 small lemon
2 tsp medium-hot curry paste
1 tbsp sesame seeds
lemon wedges, to serve

1 Remove the skin from the chicken and slash the flesh at intervals with a sharp knife.

2 Mix together the yogurt, lemon rind, lemon juice and curry paste.

3 Spread the mixture over the chicken and arrange on a foil-lined grill pan or baking sheet.

4 Place under a preheated moderately hot grill and grill for 12–15 minutes, turning once. Grill until golden brown and thoroughly cooked. Just before the end of the cooking time, sprinkle the chicken with the sesame seeds. Serve with a salad, naan bread and lemon wedges.

COOK'S VARIATION

Poppy seeds, fennel seeds or cumin seeds, or a mixture of all three, can also be used to sprinkle over the chicken.

Grilled Chicken with Pesto Toasts

This Italian-style dish is richly flavoured with pesto, which is a mixture of basil, olive oil, pine nuts and Parmesan cheese. Either red or green pesto can be used for this recipe. Passata is puréed, sieved tomatoes that you can buy in cans or jars.

Serves 4
8 part-boned chicken thighs
olive oil, for brushing
400 ml/14 fl oz passata
120 ml/4 fl oz green or red pesto sauce
12 slices French bread
90 g/3 oz freshly grated Parmesan cheese
60 g/2 oz pine nuts or flaked almonds
basil sprig, to garnish

1 Arrange the chicken in a single layer in a wide flameproof dish and brush lightly with oil. Place under a preheated grill for about 15 minutes, turning occasionally until golden brown.

2 Pierce with a skewer to ensure that the juices run clear.

3 Pour off any excess fat. Warm the passata and half the pesto sauce in a small pan and pour over the chicken. Grill for a few more minutes, turning until coated.

4 Meanwhile, spread the remaining pesto onto the slices of bread. Arrange the bread over the chicken and sprinkle with the Parmesan cheese. Scatter the pine nuts over the cheese. Grill for 2–3 minutes, until browned and bubbling. Serve hot garnished with a basil sprig.

Minty Lime Chicken

These tangy lime and honey-coated pieces have a matching sauce
or dip based on creamy natural yogurt. They could be served at a barbecue
or as a main course for a dinner party.

Serves 6
3 tbsp finely chopped mint
4 tbsp clear honey
4 tbsp lime juice
12 boneless chicken thighs
salt and pepper

SAUCE

150 g/5 oz natural thick yogurt
1 tbsp finely chopped mint
2 tsp finely grated lime rind

1 Combine the mint, honey and lime juice in a bowl.

2 Use cocktail sticks to keep the chicken thighs in neat shapes and add the chicken to the marinade, turning to coat evenly.

3 Leave to marinate for at least 30 minutes. Cook the chicken on a preheated moderately hot barbecue or grill, turning frequently and basting with the marinade. The chicken is cooked if the juices run clear when the chicken is pierced with a skewer.

4 Meanwhile, mix together the sauce ingredients.

5 Remove the cocktail sticks and serve the chicken with a salad and the sauce for dipping or pouring.

Sweet & Sour Drumsticks

Chicken drumsticks are marinated to impart a tangy, sweet and
sour flavour and a shiny glaze

Serves 4
8 chicken drumsticks
4 tbsp red wine vinegar
2 tbsp tomato purée
2 tbsp soy sauce
2tbsp clear honey
1tbsp Worcestershire sauce
1 garlic clove
good pinch cayenne
salt and pepper

1 Skin the chicken if desired and slash 2–3 times with a sharp knife.

2 Put the chicken drumsticks into a non-metallic container.

3 Mix all the remaining ingredients and pour over the chicken.

4 Leave to marinate in the refrigerator for 1 hour. Cook the drumsticks on a preheated barbecue for about 20 minutes, brushing with the marinade and turning during cooking. Serve with a crisp salad.

COOK'S TIP

For a tangy flavour, add the juice of 1 lime to the marinade. While the drumsticks are grilling, check regularly to ensure that they are not burning.

Hot & Spicy

Because chicken is popular throughout the world, there are countless spicy recipes from Asia, Mexico, south-east Asia, the Caribbean, Spain and Japan. Lime juice, coriander, fish sauce and fresh ginger root add the authentic tastes of Thailand to Thai-style Chicken Fried Rice, while Bang-Bang Chicken is a popular Szechuan dish from China with a sauce made from

peanuts and sesame seeds. From Mexico comes Enchilada Layers – tortillas stacked up with layers of tomato sauce and spicy chicken, and Chicken Fajitas – chicken spiked with hot chillies, served in tortillas, and topped with soured cream, red onion and limes. Add Margueritas and you have a tasty Mexican spread. Baby Chickens with Green Peppercorns is a creative modern dish that would be perfect for any special occasion. It is served with rice cooked in a tasty sauce of peppercorns, mustard and wine.

Bang-Bang Chicken

The cooked chicken meat is tenderized by being pounded with a rolling pin,
hence the name for this very popular Szechuan dish from China.

Serves 4

1 litre/1³/₄ pints water
2 chicken quarters (breast half and leg)
1 cucumber,
cut into matchstick shreds

SAUCE

2 tbsp light soy sauce
1 tsp sugar
1 tbsp finely chopped
spring onion
1 tsp red chilli oil
¹/₄ tsp pepper
1 tsp white sesame seeds
2 tbsp peanut butter, creamed
with a little sesame oil

1 Bring the water to a rolling boil in a
wok or a large saucepan. Add the
chicken pieces, reduce the heat, cover
and cook for 30–35 minutes.

2 Remove the chicken from the pan
and immerse it in a bowl of cold
water for at least 1 hour to cool it,
ready for shredding.

3 Remove the chicken pieces and
drain well. Pat dry with paper towels,
then take the meat off the bone.

4 On a flat surface, pound the
chicken with a rolling pin, then tear
the meat into shreds with two forks.
Mix with the shredded cucumber and
arrange in a serving dish.

5 To serve, mix together all the sauce
ingredients and pour over the chicken
and cucumber.

Thai-Style Chicken Fried Rice

A few special ingredients give this rice dish an authentic Thai flavour.

Serves 4
250 g/8 oz
white long-grain rice
4 tbsp vegetable oil
2 garlic cloves, chopped finely
6 shallots, sliced finely
1 red pepper,
deseeded and diced
125 g/4 oz French beans,
cut into 2.5 cm/1 inch lengths
1 tbsp Thai red curry paste
350 g/12 oz cooked skinless,
boneless chicken, chopped
$^1/_2$ tsp ground coriander seeds
1 tsp finely grated fresh ginger root
2 tbsp Thai fish sauce
finely grated rind of 1 lime
3 tbsp lime juice
1 tbsp chopped fresh coriander
salt and pepper

TO GARNISH

lime wedges
sprigs of fresh coriander

1 Cook the rice in plenty of boiling, lightly salted water for 12–15 minutes until tender. Drain, rinse in cold water and drain thoroughly.

2 Heat the oil in a large frying pan or wok and add the garlic and shallots. Fry gently for 2–3 minutes until golden.

3 Add the pepper and French beans and stir-fry for 2 minutes. Add the Thai curry paste and stir-fry for 1 minute.

4 Add the cooked rice to the pan, then the chicken, ground coriander, ginger, fish sauce, lime rind and juice, and fresh coriander. Stir-fry over a medium-high heat for about 4–5 minutes, until the rice and chicken are thoroughly reheated. Season to taste.

5 Garnish with lime wedges and coriander before serving.

Chicken Fajitas

This spicy chicken filling, made with mixed peppers, chillies and mushrooms and strongly flavoured with lime, is served in folded tortillas and topped with soured cream.
Many other fillings can be used – the possibilities are endless.

Serves 4
2 red peppers
2 green peppers
2 tbsp olive oil
2 onions, chopped
3 garlic cloves, crushed
1 chilli, deseeded and chopped finely
2 skinless, boneless chicken breasts, about 350 g/12 oz
60 g/2 oz button mushrooms, sliced
2 tsp chopped fresh coriander
grated rind of $1/2$ lime
2 tbsp lime juice
4 wheat or corn tortillas
4–6 tbsp soured cream
salt and pepper

TO GARNISH

sliced red onion

chopped tomatoes

lime wedges

1 Halve the peppers, remove the seeds and place skin-side upwards under a preheated moderate grill until well charred. Leave to cool slightly and then peel off the skin. Cut the flesh into thin slices.

2 Heat the oil in a pan, add the onions, garlic and chilli, and fry gently for a few minutes until the onion has softened.

3 Cut the chicken into narrow strips. Add to the vegetable mixture in the pan and fry for 4–5 minutes until almost cooked, stirring occasionally.

4 Add the peppers, mushrooms, coriander, lime rind and juice, and continue to cook for 2–3 minutes. Season to taste.

5 Heat the tortillas, wrapped in foil, in a preheated oven, 180°C/350°F/ Gas Mark 4, for a few minutes. Bend the tortillas in half and divide the chicken mixture between them evenly.

6 Top the chicken filling with a spoonful of soured cream. Serve garnished with red onion slices, chopped tomatoes and lime wedges.

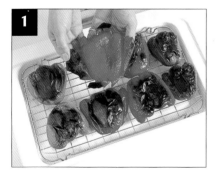

Enchilada Layers

You can vary the filling for these layered Mexican tortillas by using beef,
fish or shellfish. If preferred, the tortillas can be rolled up once they are filled,
rather than baking them in layers.

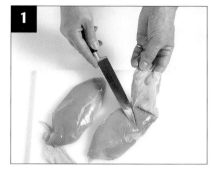

Serves 4
500 g/1 lb boneless chicken breasts
2 tbsp olive oil
1 large onion, sliced thinly
3 garlic cloves, crushed
1 tsp ground cumin seeds
2 tbsp stock or water
1 tbsp chopped fresh coriander
6 wheat or corn tortillas
175 g/6 oz feta cheese, coarsely grated
salt and pepper
sprigs of fresh coriander to garnish

TOMATO SAUCE

2 tbsp oil
1 onion, chopped very finely
3 garlic cloves, crushed
1 red chilli, chopped finely
425 g/14 oz can chopped tomatoes with herbs
200 g/7 oz can chopped tomatoes
3 tbsp tomato purée
2 tbsp lime juice
2 tsp caster sugar
salt and pepper

1 Remove the skin from the chicken
and chop finely. Heat the oil and fry
the onion and garlic until softened.

2 Add the chicken and fry for 5
minutes. Add the cumin and stock.
Cook for 3 minutes until tender. Add
the coriander. Remove from the heat.

3 To make the tomato sauce, heat the
oil and fry the onion, garlic and chilli
gently until softened.

4 Add all the tomatoes, the tomato
purée, lime juice, sugar and seasoning.
Simmer gently for 10 minutes.

5 Cover a tortilla with a fifth of the
chicken mixture and 2 tablespoons of
the tomato sauce, then sprinkle with
grated cheese. Continue to layer in

this way, finishing with cheese.
6 Place the layered enchiladas in an
uncovered dish in a preheated oven,
190°C/375°F/Gas Mark 5, for 25
minutes, or until the top is lightly
browned. Serve in wedges, garnished
with a sprig of coriander.

Chicken Paprika

Paprika, caraway seeds and soured cream give this dish an Eastern European flavour.
Paprika is a seasoning commonly used in Hungary.

Serves 4
60 g/2 oz butter
4 chicken quarters
1 tbsp paprika
1 tbsp caraway seeds
1 onion, chopped finely
1 clove garlic, crushed
1 red pepper, finely chopped
125 g/4 oz mushrooms, chopped finely
125 g/4 oz pancetta, or smoked streaky bacon, diced
75 ml/3 fl oz sherry
150 ml/$\frac{1}{4}$ pint soured cream
1 tbsp cornflour
salt and pepper

1 Heat the butter in a frying pan, add the chicken and brown well on all sides. Stir in the paprika and caraway seeds and season. Remove the chicken and set aside.

2 Add the onion and garlic to the pan and soften in the butter for about 10 minutes. Transfer the chicken and onions to a baking dish, cover and transfer to a preheated oven, 200°C/400°F/Gas Mark 6. Bake for 40 minutes, turning once or twice.

3 Remove the chicken and onions from the dish, reserving the cooking juices. Set aside to keep warm. Pour the cooking juices into a large frying pan set over a moderate heat.

4 Stir in the pepper, mushroom and pancetta, and fry for 15 minutes.

5 Add the sherry, and simmer until reduced. Season to taste.

6 To finish the sauce, combine the soured cream and cornflour and stir into the pan until the sauce is smooth and thick. Adjust the seasoning and serve the sauce with the chicken pieces.

Chicken with Mushrooms

Try to find Chinese straw mushrooms for this dish. When cooked they are
brown and slippery and make a delicious addition to the chicken.

Serves 4

300–350 g/10–12 oz skinless,
boneless chicken

$^1/_2$ tsp sugar

1 tbsp light soy sauce

1 tsp rice wine or dry sherry

2 tsp cornflour

4–6 dried Chinese
mushrooms, soaked in
warm water and drained

1 tbsp finely shredded fresh
ginger root

a few drops of sesame oil

salt and pepper

coriander leaves,
to garnish

1 Cut the chicken into small bite-sized pieces and place in a bowl. Add the sugar, soy sauce, wine and cornflour and leave to marinate for 25–30 minutes.

2 Dry the mushrooms on paper towels. Slice into thin shreds, discarding any hard pieces of stem.

3 Place the chicken pieces on a heat-proof dish that will fit inside a bamboo steamer. Arrange the mushroom and ginger shreds on top of the chicken and sprinkle with sesame oil, and salt and pepper.

4 Place the dish on the rack inside a hot steamer or on a rack in a wok or large frying pan filled with hot water. Steam over high heat for 20 minutes. Serve hot, garnished with coriander leaves.

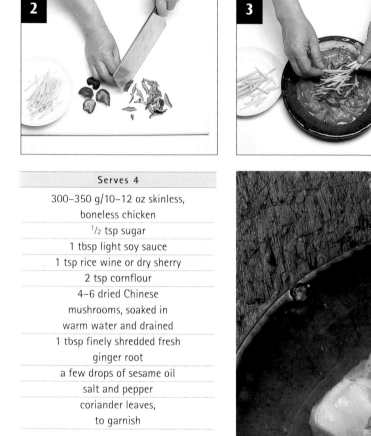

Quick Chinese Chicken with Noodles

Chicken and fresh vegetables are flavoured with ginger and Chinese five-spice powder in this quick and easy stir-fry. Vary the vegetables according to what is in season and make sure that they are as fresh as possible.

Serves 4
175 g/6 oz Chinese thread egg noodles
2 tbsp sesame or vegetable oil
30 g/1 oz peanuts
1 bunch of spring onions, sliced
1 green pepper, cut into thin strips
1 large carrot, cut into matchstick strips
125 g/4 oz cauliflower, broken into small florets
350 g/12 oz skinless, boneless chicken, cut into strips
250 g/8 oz mushrooms, sliced
1 tsp finely grated fresh ginger root
1 tsp Chinese five-spice powder
1 tbsp chopped fresh coriander
1 tbsp light soy sauce
salt and pepper
fresh chives, to garnish

1 Put the noodles into a large bowl and cover with boiling water. Leave to soak for 6 minutes, or according to the instructions on the packet.

2 Meanwhile, heat the oil in a wok or large frying pan. Add the peanuts and stir-fry for about 1 minute until browned. Lift the peanuts out with a perforated spoon and drain on paper towels.

3 Add the spring onions, pepper, carrot, cauliflower and chicken strips to the pan. Stir-fry over a high heat for 4–5 minutes, until the chicken is cooked thoroughly. The vegetables should be still crisp, bright and colourful.

4 Drain the noodles thoroughly and add them to the wok. Add the mushrooms and stir-fry for 2 minutes. Add the ginger, five-spice powder and coriander and stir-fry for another minute.

5 Season with the soy sauce, and salt and pepper. Sprinkle with the peanuts, garnish with chives and serve at once on warmed plates.

Lime & Coriander Chicken Fried Rice

Lime rind and lime juice are combined with chopped fresh coriander
to give this dish a lively Thai flavour.

Serves 4
250 g/8 oz
long-grain white rice
4 tbsp vegetable oil
2 garlic cloves, chopped finely
1 small green chilli, deseeded and chopped finely
5 shallots, sliced finely
1 tbsp Thai green curry paste
1 yellow or green pepper, chopped
2 celery sticks, sliced finely
250 g/8 oz cooked skinless, boneless chicken, chopped
2 tbsp light soy sauce
finely grated rind of 1 lime
2 tbsp lime juice
1 tbsp chopped fresh coriander
30 g/1 oz unsalted peanuts, toasted

TO GARNISH

sprigs of fresh coriander
finely sliced shallots
lime slices

1 Cook the rice in plenty of boiling, lightly salted water for about 12 minutes, until tender. Drain, rinse with cold water and drain thoroughly.

2 Heat the oil in a wok or large frying pan and add the garlic. Fry gently for 2 minutes until golden. Add the chilli and shallots, and cook, stirring, for a further 3–4 minutes until slightly softened.

3 Add the Thai curry paste to the wok or frying pan and fry for 1 minute, then add the yellow or green pepper and the celery. Stir-fry briskly for 2 minutes.

4 Add the cooked rice to the wok or frying pan and add the chicken, soy sauce, lime rind and juice, and coriander. Stir-fry over a medium-high heat for 4–5 minutes, until the rice and chicken are heated.

5 Serve sprinkled with peanuts. Garnish with sprigs of fresh coriander, shallots and lime slices.

Baby Chickens with Peppercorns

Baby chickens are a good alternative to chicken. One bird serves two people and can be cooked whole. Sautéed cherry tomatoes are a colourful accompaniment.

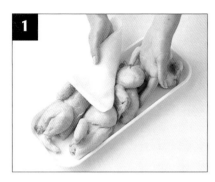

Serves 4
2 baby chickens, halved, washed and dried
2 tbsp oil
30 g/1 oz butter
1 onion, chopped
3 tbsp bottled green peppercorns
2 tbsp wholegrain mustard
120 ml/4 fl oz white wine
200 g/7 oz basmati and wild rice
500 ml/16 fl oz chicken stock
salt and pepper

1 Wash the chickens and pat dry. Heat the oil and butter, and cook the onion for 5 minutes until softened.

2 Season the chickens well with salt and pepper, and add to the pan. Brown all over then transfer to a baking sheet.

3 Finish cooking the baby chickens in a preheated oven, 200°C/400°F/Gas Mark 6, for 30 minutes.

4 Meanwhile, stir the peppercorns, mustard and wine into the pan juices, bring to the boil and reduce by half.

5 Stir in the rice, and pour on the stock. Season well and bring to a simmer. Cook for 18–20 minutes. Adjust the seasoning, if necessary.

6 Serve the baby chickens piping hot on a bed of rice.

Kashmiri Chicken

This warming, rich and spicy dish is based on the traditional cooking style of Northern India, using chicken on the bone. If you prefer, use boneless chicken breasts instead of legs, and cut into large chunks for cooking.

Serves 4
4 skinless chicken drumsticks
4 skinless chicken thighs
150 ml/^{1}/$_4$ pint
natural yogurt
4 tbsp Tikka curry paste
2 tbsp sunflower oil
1 medium onion, sliced thinly
1 garlic clove, crushed
1 tsp ground cumin
1 tsp finely chopped fresh
ginger root
^{1}/$_2$ tsp chilli paste
4 tsp chicken stock
2 tbsp ground almonds
salt
fresh coriander,
to garnish

1 Slash the chicken fairly deeply at intervals with a sharp knife and place in a large bowl.

2 Mix together the yogurt and curry paste and stir into the chicken tossing to coat evenly. Cover and chill for at least 1 hour.

3 Heat the oil in a large pan and fry the onion and garlic for 4–5 minutes until softened but not browned.

4 Stir in the cumin, ginger and chilli paste and cook gently for 1 minute.

5 Add the chicken pieces and fry gently, turning occasionally, for about 10 minutes or until evenly browned. Stir in any remaining marinade with the stock and almonds. Cover the pan and simmer gently for a further 15 minutes or until the chicken is completely cooked and tender.

6 Season to taste with a little salt. Garnish the chicken with coriander and serve with pilau rice, pickles and poppadums.

Teppanyaki

This simple, Japanese style of cooking is ideal for thinly sliced breast of chicken.
Mirin is a rich, sweet rice wine which you can buy in oriental shops, but if it is not
available add one tablespoon of soft light brown sugar to the sauce instead.

Serves 4
4 boneless chicken breasts
1 red pepper
1 green pepper
4 spring onions
8 baby corn cobs
100g/4 oz bean-sprouts
1 tbsp sesame or sunflower oil
4 tbsp soy sauce
4 tbsp mirin
1 tbsp grated fresh ginger root

1 Remove the skin from the chicken and slice at a slight angle, to a thickness of about 5 mm/¼ inch.

2 Deseed and thinly slice the peppers and trim and slice the spring onions and corn cobs. Arrange the peppers, spring onions, corn and bean-sprouts on a plate with the sliced chicken.

3 Heat a large griddle or heavy frying pan then lightly brush with oil. Add the vegetables and chicken slices in small batches, allowing space between them so that they cook thoroughly.

4 Combine the soy sauce, mirin and ginger and serve as a dip with the chicken and vegetables.

Spanish Chicken with Prawns

This unusual dish, with its mixture of chicken and shellfish, is typically Spanish.
The basis of this recipe is sofrito: a slow-cooked mixture of onion and tomato in olive oil, with garlic and peppers.
Chorizo, a cooked, spicy Spanish sausage, is also used in this recipe.

Serves 4
4 chicken quarters
1 tbsp olive oil
1 red pepper
1 medium onion
2 garlic cloves, crushed
425 g/14 oz can chopped tomatoes
200 ml/7 fl oz dry white wine
4 tbsp chopped fresh oregano
125 g/4 oz chorizo sausage
125 g/4 oz peeled prawns
salt and pepper

1 Remove the skin from the chicken. Heat the oil in a wide, heavy pan and fry the chicken, turning occasionally until golden brown.

2 Deseed and slice the pepper and peel and slice the onion. Add to the pan and fry gently to soften.

3 Add the garlic with the tomatoes, wine and oregano. Season well, then bring to the boil, cover and simmer gently for 45 minutes or until the chicken is tender and the juices run clear when the chicken is pierced with a skewer.

4 Thinly slice the chorizo and add with the prawns, then simmer for a further 5 minutes. Season to taste and serve with rice.

Regal Chicken with Cashew Nut Stuffing

Most of the flavourful stuffing is cooked separately from the chicken, only a small amount is added to the neck end.

Serves 4
1 chicken, weighing about 1.5 kg/3 lb
1 small onion, halved
30 g/1 oz butter, melted
1 tsp ground turmeric
1 tsp ground ginger
1/2 tsp cayenne
salt and pepper
fresh coriander, to garnish

STUFFING

2 tbsp oil
1 medium onion, chopped finely
1/2 medium red pepper, chopped finely
2 garlic cloves, crushed
125 g/4 oz basmati rice
350 ml/12 fl oz hot chicken stock
grated rind 1/2 lemon
1/2 tsp ground turmeric
1/2 tsp ground ginger
1/2 tsp ground coriander
pinch cayenne pepper
90 g/3 oz salted cashew nuts, a little chopped pepper

1 To make the stuffing, heat the oil in a saucepan, add the onion, red pepper and garlic and cook gently for 4–5 minutes. Add the rice and stir to coat with the oil. Add the stock, bring to the boil, then simmer for 15 minutes until all the liquid is absorbed. Transfer to a bowl and add the remaining ingredients for the stuffing. Season well with pepper.

2 Place half the stuffing in the neck end of the chicken and secure with a cocktail stick. Put the halved onion into the cavity of the chicken.

3 Spoon the rest of the rice stuffing into a greased ovenproof dish and cover with foil.

4 Place the chicken in a roasting tin. Prick all over avoiding the stuffed

area. Mix the butter and spices, season, then brush over the chicken.

5 Roast in a preheated oven, 190°C/375°F/Gas Mark 5, for 1 hour, basting from time to time. Place the dish of rice stuffing in the oven and continue to cook the chicken for another 30 minutes. Remove the cocktail stick and serve the chicken with stuffing and gravy.

Mexican Chicken

Chilli, tomatoes and corn are typical ingredients
in a Mexican dish.

Serves 4
2 tbsp oil
8 chicken drumsticks
1 medium onion, finely chopped
1 tsp chilli powder
1 tsp ground coriander
425 g/14 oz can chopped tomatoes
2 tbsp tomato purée
125 g/4 oz frozen sweetcorn
salt and pepper

1 Heat the oil in a large frying pan, add the chicken drumsticks and cook over a medium heat until lightly browned. Remove from the pan and set aside.

2 Add the onion to the pan and cook for 3–4 minutes until soft, then stir in the chilli powder and coriander and cook for a few seconds. Add the chopped tomatoes with their juice and the tomato purée.

3 Return the chicken to the pan and simmer gently for 20 minutes until the chicken is tender and thoroughly cooked. Add the sweetcorn and cook a further 3–4 minutes. Season to taste.

4 Serve with rice and mixed pepper salad.

Golden Chicken Pilau

This is a simple version of a creamy textured and mildly spiced Indian pilau. Although there are lots of ingredients, there's very little preparation needed for this dish.

Serves 4
60 g/2 oz butter
8 skinless, boneless chicken thighs, cut into large pieces
1 medium onion, sliced
1 tsp ground turmeric
1tsp ground cinnamon
250 g/8 oz long grain rice
450 ml/³/₄ pint natural yogurt
60 g/2 oz sultanas
200 ml/7 fl oz stock
1 medium tomato, chopped
2 tbsp chopped fresh coriander or parsley
2 tbsp toasted coconut
salt and pepper
fresh coriander, to garnish

1 Heat the butter in a heavy or non-stick pan and fry the chicken with the onion for about 3 minutes.

2 Stir in the turmeric, cinnamon, rice and seasoning and fry gently for 3 minutes.

3 Add the yogurt, sultanas and stock and mix well. Cover and simmer for 10 minutes, stirring occasionally until the rice is tender and the stock has all been absorbed.

4 Add the tomato and coriander to the pilau. Sprinkle with the toasted coconut and garnish with fresh coriander.

Chilli Coconut Chicken

This tasty Thai-style dish has a classic sauce of lime, peanut, coconut and chilli.
You'll find coconut cream in most supermarkets or delicatessens.

Serves 4
30 g/1 oz coconut cream
150 ml/¼ pint hot chicken stock
1 tbsp sunflower oil
8 skinless, boneless chicken thighs, cut into long, thin strips
1 small red chilli, sliced thinly
4 spring onions, sliced thinly
4 tbsp smooth or crunchy peanut butter
finely grated rind and juice of 1 lime
2 tbsp chopped fresh coriander (optional)

1 Dissolve the coconut cream in the chicken stock.

2 Heat the oil in a wok or large heavy pan and fry the chicken, stirring, until golden. Stir in the chilli and onions and cook gently for a few minutes.

3 Add the peanut butter, coconut cream, lime rind and juice and simmer uncovered, stirring, for about 5 minutes. Serve with boiled rice and sprinkle with coriander, if using.

COOK'S VARIATION

Serve jasmine rice with this spicy dish. It has a fragrant aroma that is well-suited to Thai-style recipes.

Chicken in Red Pepper & Almond Sauce

This tasty chicken dish combines warm spices and almonds and is spiked with anise.

Serves 4
30 g/1 oz butter
7 tbsp vegetable oil
4 skinless, boneless chicken breasts, cut into 4cm/2 inch x 2 cm/1 inch pieces
1 medium onion, roughly chopped
2 cm/1 inch piece fresh ginger root
3 garlic cloves, peeled
30 g/1 oz blanched almonds
1 large red pepper, roughly chopped
1 tbsp ground cumin
2 tsp ground coriander
1 tsp ground turmeric
pinch cayenne pepper
1/2 tsp salt
150 ml/1/4 pint water
3 star anise
2 tbsp lemon juice
pepper

1 Heat the butter and 1 tablespoon of oil in a frying pan, add the chicken pieces and cook for 5 minutes. Transfer the chicken to a plate.

2 Combine the onion, ginger, garlic, almonds, red pepper, cumin, coriander, turmeric, cayenne and salt in a food processor or liquidiser. Blend to a smooth paste.

3 Heat the remaining oil in a large saucepan or deep frying pan. Add the paste and fry for 10–12 minutes.

4 Add the chicken pieces, the water, star anise, lemon juice and pepper. Cover, reduce the heat and simmer gently for 25 minutes or until the chicken is tender. Stir a few times during cooking.

Cajun Chicken Gumbo

This complete main course is cooked in one saucepan for simplicity. If you're cooking for one, simply halve the ingredients; the cooking time should stay the same. The whole chilli makes the dish hot and spicy – if you prefer a milder flavour, discard the seeds of the chilli.

Serves 2
1 tbsp sunflower oil
4 chicken thighs
1 small onion, diced
2 sticks celery, diced
1 small green pepper, diced
90 g/3 oz long grain rice
300 ml/$\frac{1}{2}$ pint chicken stock
1 small red chilli
250 g/8 oz okra
15ml/1 tbsp tomato purée
salt and pepper

1 Heat the oil in a wide pan and fry the chicken until golden. Remove the chicken from the pan. Stir in the onion, celery and pepper and fry for 1 minute. Pour off any excess fat.

2 Add the rice and fry, stirring for a further minute. Add the stock and heat until boiling.

3 Thinly slice the chilli and trim the okra. Add to the pan with the tomato purée. Season to taste.

4 Return the chicken to the pan and stir. Cover tightly and simmer gently for 15 minutes, or until the rice is tender, the chicken is thoroughly cooked and the liquid absorbed. Stir occasionally and if it becomes too dry, add a little extra stock to moisten.

Cumin Spiced Apricot Chicken

Spiced chicken legs are partially boned and packed with dried apricots for an intense fruity flavour. A golden, spiced, low-fat yogurt coating keeps the chicken moist and tender.

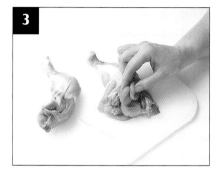

Serves 4
4 large, skinless chicken leg quarters
finely grated rind of 1 lemon
200 g/7 oz ready-to-eat dried apricots
1 tbsp ground cumin
1 tsp ground turmeric
125 g/4 oz low-fat natural yogurt
salt and pepper

TO SERVE

250 g/8 oz brown rice
2 tbsp flaked hazelnuts or almonds, toasted
2 tbsp sunflower seeds, toasted

1 Remove any excess fat from the chicken legs. Use a small sharp knife to carefully cut the flesh away from the thigh bone.

2 Scrape the meat away down as far as the knuckle. Grasp the thigh bone firmly and twist it to break it away from the drumstick.

3 Open out the boned part of the chicken and sprinkle with lemon rind and pepper. Pack the dried apricots into each piece of chicken.

4 Fold over to enclose, and secure with cocktail sticks. Mix together the cumin, turmeric, yogurt and salt and pepper, then brush this mixture over the chicken to coat evenly. Place the chicken in an ovenproof dish or

roasting tin and bake in a preheated oven, 190°C/375°F/Gas Mark 5, for 35–40 minutes, or until the chicken juices run clear, not pink, when pierced through the thickest part with a skewer.

5 Meanwhile, cook the rice in boiling, lightly salted water until just tender, then drain well. Stir the hazelnuts and sunflower seeds into the rice and serve with the chicken.

Chicken with Peppers & Black Bean Sauce

This tasty chicken stir-fry is quick and easy to make and is full of fresh flavours and crunchy vegetables.

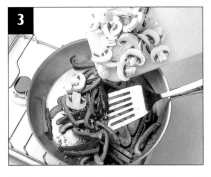

Serves 4

425 g/14 oz chicken breasts, sliced thinly
pinch of cornflour
2 tbsp oil
1 garlic clove, crushed
1 tbsp black bean sauce
1 each small red and green pepper, cut into strips
1 red chilli, chopped finely
75 g/3 oz mushrooms, sliced
1 onion, chopped
6 spring onions, chopped
salt and pepper

SEASONING

$^1/_2$ tsp salt
$^1/_2$ tsp sugar
3 tbsp chicken stock
1 tbsp dark soy sauce
2 tbsp beef stock
2 tbsp rice wine
1 tsp cornflour, blended with a little rice wine

1 Put the chicken strips in a bowl. Add a pinch of salt and a pinch of cornflour and cover with water. Leave to stand for 30 minutes.

2 Heat 1 tablespoon of the oil in a wok or deep-sided frying pan and stir-fry the chicken for 4 minutes. Remove the chicken to a warm serving dish and clean the wok or pan.

3 Add the remaining oil to the wok and add the garlic, black bean sauce, green and red peppers, chilli, mushrooms, onion and spring onions.

Stir fry for 2 minutes then return the chicken to the wok.

4 Add the seasoning ingredients, fry for 3 minutes and thicken with a little cornflour. Serve with fresh noodles.

COOK'S TIP

Black bean sauce can be found in specialist shops and in many supermarkets. Use dried noodles if you can't find fresh noodles.

Thai Stir-Fried Chicken with Vegetables

Coconut adds a creamy texture and delicious flavour to this
Thai-style stir-fry, which is spiked with green chilli.

Serves 4
3 tbsp sesame oil
350 g/12 oz chicken breast, sliced thinly
8 shallots, sliced
2 garlic cloves, finely chopped
2.5cm/1 inch piece fresh root ginger, grated
1 green chilli, finely chopped
1 each red and green pepper, sliced thinly
3 courgettes, thinly sliced
2 tbsp ground almonds
1 tsp ground cinnamon
1 tbsp oyster sauce
50 g/2 oz creamed coconut, grated
salt and pepper

1 Heat the sesame oil in a wok, add the chicken, season, and stir fry for about 4 minutes.

2 Add the shallots, garlic, ginger and chilli and stir-fry for 2 minutes.

3 Add the peppers and courgettes and cook for about 1 minute.

4 Finally, add the ground almonds, cinnamon, oyster sauce and coconut. Stir fry for 1 minute and serve immediately.

Fruity Garlic Curried Chicken

Serve this fruity curry with mango chutney and naan bread, and top the curry
with seedless grapes. Mango or pears make a good substitute for pineapple.

Serves 4–6
1 tbsp oil
900 g/1³/₄ lb chicken meat, chopped
60 g/2 oz flour, seasoned
32 shallots, roughly chopped
4 garlic cloves, crushed with a little olive oil
3 cooking apples, diced
1 pineapple, diced
125 g/4 oz sultanas
1 tbsp clear honey
300 ml/¹/₂ pint chicken stock
2 tbsp Worcestershire sauce
3 tbsp hot curry paste
150 ml/¹/₄ pint soured cream
salt and pepper

1 Heat the oil in a large frying pan.
Coat the meat in the seasoned flour
and cook for about 4 minutes until it
is browned all over. Transfer the
chicken to a large deep casserole.

2 Slowly fry the shallots, garlic,
apples, pineapple and sultanas in the
pan juices.

3 Add the chicken stock, seasoning,
Worcestershire sauce and curry paste.

4 Pour the sauce over the chicken
and cover the casserole with a lid or
cooking foil.

5 Cook in the centre of a preheated
oven, 180°C/350°F/Gas Mark 4,
for 2 hours. Stir in the soured cream
and cook for a further 15 minutes.
Serve with rice.

Index